FIELDS
OF VICTORY

Mrs. Humphry Ward

1st WORLD
LIBRARY
Literary Society

Fields of Victory

Mrs. Humphry Ward

© 1st World Library, 2006
PO Box 2211
Fairfield, IA 52556
www.1stworldlibrary.com
First Edition

LCCN: 2006937829

Softcover ISBN: 978-1-4218-3353-8
Hardcover ISBN: 978-1-4218-3253-1
eBook ISBN: 978-1-4218-3453-5

Purchase *"Fields of Victory"*
as a traditional bound book at:
www.1stWorldLibrary.com/purchase.asp?ISBN=978-1-4218-3353-8

1st World Library is a literary, educational organization
dedicated to:

- Creating a free internet library of downloadable ebooks

- Hosting writing competitions and offering book
publishing scholarships.

Interested in more 1st World Library books?
contact: literacy@1stworldlibrary.com
Check us out at: www.1stworldlibrary.com

1st World Library Literary Society

Giving Back to the World

"If you want to work on the core problem, it's early school literacy."

- James Barksdale, former CEO of Netscape

"No skill is more crucial to the future of a child, or to a democratic and prosperous society, than literacy."

- Los Angeles Times

Literacy... means far more than learning how to read and write... The aim is to transmit... knowledge and promote social participation."

- UNESCO

"Literacy is not a luxury, it is a right and a responsibility. If our world is to meet the challenges of the twenty-first century we must harness the energy and creativity of all our citizens."

- President Bill Clinton

"Parents should be encouraged to read to their children, and teachers should be equipped with all available techniques for teaching literacy, so the varying needs and capacities of individual kids can be taken into account."

- Hugh Mackay

CONTENTS

A WORD OF INTRODUCTION

May 26th.

It is a bold thing, I fear, to offer the public yet more letters based on a journey through the battle-fields of France—especially at a moment when impressions are changing so fast, when the old forms of writing about the war seem naturally out of date, or even distasteful, and the new are not yet born. Yet perhaps in this intermediate period, the impressions of one who made two journeys over some of the same ground in 1916 and 1917, while the great struggle was at its height, and on this third occasion found herself on the Western front just two months after the Armistice, may not be unwelcome to those who, like myself, feel the need of detaching as soon as possible some general and consistent ideas from the infinite complexity, the tragic and bewildering detail, of the past four years. The motive which sent me to France three months ago was the wish to make clear to myself if I could, and thereby to others, the true measure of the part played by the British Empire and the British Armies in the concluding campaigns of the war. I knew that if it could be done at all at the present moment—and by myself—it could only be done in a very broad and summary way; and also that its only claim to value would lie in its being a faithful report, within the limits I had set myself, of the opinions of those who were actually at the heart of things, *i.e.*, of the British Higher Command, and of individual officers who had taken an active part in the war. For the view taken in these pages of last year's campaigns, I have had, of course, the three great despatches of the British Commander-in-Chief on which to base the general sketch I had in mind; but in addition I have had much kind help from the British Headquarters in France, where officers of the General Staff were still working when I paid a wintry visit to the famous Ecole Militaire at the end of January; supplemented since my return to London by assistance from other distinguished soldiers now at the War Office, who have taken trouble to help me, for which I can never thank them enough.[1] It was, naturally, the aim of the little book which won it sympathy; the fact that it was an attempt to carry to its natural end, in brief compass, the story which, at Mr. Roosevelt's suggestion, I first tried to tell in *England's Effort*, published in 1916. *England's Effort* was a bird's-eye view of the first two years of the war, of the gathering of the new Armies, of the passing into law, and the results—up to the Battle of the Somme—of the Munitions Act of 1915. In this book, which I have again thrown into the form of letters—(it was, in fact, written week by week for transmission to America after my return home from France)—I have confined myself to the events of last year, and with the special object of determining what ultimate effect upon the war was produced by that vast military development of Great Britain and the Empire, in which Lord Kitchener took the first memorable steps. It seemed to me, at the end of last year, as to many others, that owing, perhaps, to the prominence of certain startling or picturesque episodes in the history of 1918, the overwhelming and decisive influence of the British Armies on the last stage of the struggle had been to some extent obscured and misunderstood even amongst ourselves—still more, and very naturally, amongst our Allies. Not, of course, by any of those in close contact with the actual march of the war, and its directing forces; but rather by that floating public opinion, now more intelligent, now more ignorant, which plays so largely on us all, whether through conversation or the press.

[1] My thanks are especially due to Lieut.-Colonel Boraston, of the General Staff, and also to my friend Colonel John Buchan, whose wonderful knowledge of the war, as shown in his History, has done so much during the

last four years to keep the public at home in touch with all the forces of the Allies, but especially with the British Armies and the British Navy, throughout the whole course of the struggle.

My object, then, was to bring out as clearly as I could the part that the British Armies in France, including, of course, the great Dominion contingents, played in the fighting of last year. To do so, it was necessary also to try and form some opinion as to the respective shares in the final result of the three great Armies at work in France in 1918; to put the effort of Great Britain, that is, in its due relation to the whole concluding act of the war. In making such an attempt I am very conscious of its audacity; and I need not say that it would be a cause of sharp regret to me should the estimate here given—which is, of course, the estimate of an Englishwoman—offend any French or American friend of mine. The justice and generosity of the best French opinion on the war has been conspicuously shown on many recent occasions; while the speech in Paris the other day of the If Dean of Harvard as to the relative parts in the war—on French soil—of the Big Three—and the reception given to it by an audience of American officers have, I venture to think, stirred and deepened affection for America in the heart of those English persons who read the report of a remarkable meeting. But there is still much ignorance both here at home and among our Allies, on both sides of the sea, of the full part played by the forces of the British Empire in last year's drama. So it seemed to me, at least, when I was travelling, a few months ago, over some of the battle-fields of 1918; and I came home with a full heart, determined to tell the story—the last chapter in *England's Effort*—broadly and sincerely, as I best could; It was my firm confidence throughout the writing of these letters that the friendship between Britain, France, and America—a friendship on which, in my belief, rests the future happiness and peace of the world—can only gain from free speech and from the free comparison of opinion. And in the brilliant final despatch of Sir Douglas Haig which appeared on April 12th, after six letters had been written and sent to America, will be found, I venture to suggest, the full and authoritative exposition of some at least of the main lines of thought I have so imperfectly summarised in this little book.

The ten letters were written at intervals between February and May. It seemed better, in republishing them, not to attempt much recasting. They represent, mainly, the impressions of a journey, and of the conversations and reading to which it led. I have left them very much, therefore, in their original form, hoping that at least the freshness of "things seen" may atone somewhat for their many faults.

CHAPTER I

FRANCE UNDER THE ARMISTICE

London, *February, 1919.*

A bewildering three weeks spent in a perpetually changing scene—changing, and yet, outside Paris, in its essential elements terribly the same—that is how my third journey to France, since the war began, appears to me as I look back upon it. My dear daughter-secretary and I have motored during January some nine hundred miles through the length and breadth of France, some of it in severe weather. We have spent some seven days on the British front, about the same on the French front, with a couple of nights at Metz, and a similar time at Strasburg, and rather more than a week in Paris. Little enough! But what a time of crowding and indelible impressions! Now, sitting in this quiet London house, I seem to be still bending forward in the motor-car, which became a sort of home to us, looking out, so intently that one's eyes suffered, at the unrolling scene. I still see the grim desolation of the Ypres salient; the heaps of ugly wreck that men call Lens and Lieviny and Souchez; and that long line of Notre Dame de Lorette, with the Bois de Bouvigny to the west of it—where I stood among Canadian batteries just six weeks before the battle of Arras in 1917. The lamentable ruin of once beautiful Arras, the desolation of Douai, and the villages between it and Valenciennes, the wanton destruction of what was once the heart of Cambrai, and that grim scene of the broken bridge on the Cambrai—Bapaume road, over the Canal du Nord, where we got out on a sombre afternoon, to look and look again at a landscape that will be famous through the world for generations: they rise again, with the sharpness of no ordinary recollection, on the inward vision. So too Bourlon Wood, high and dark against the evening sky; the unspeakable desolation and ruin of the road thence to Bapaume; Bapaume itself, under the moon, its poor huddled heaps lit only, as we walked about it, by that strange, tranquil light from overhead, and the lamps of our standing motor-car; some dim shapes and sights emerging on the long and thrice-famous road from Bapaume to Albert, first, the dark mound of the Butte de Warlencourt, with three white crosses on its top, and once a mysterious light in a fragment of a ruined house, the only light I saw on the whole long downward stretch from Bapaume to Albert. Then the church of Albert, where the hanging Virgin used to be in 1917, hovering above a town that for all the damage done to it was then still a town of living men, and is now a place so desolate that one shrinks from one's own voice in the solitude, and so wrecked that only the traffic directions here and there, writ large, seem to guide us through the shapeless heaps that once were streets. And, finally, the scanty lights of Amiens, marking the end of the first part of our journey.

These were the sights of the first half of our journey. And as they recur to me, I understand so well the anxious and embittered mood of France, which was so evident a month ago;[2] though now, I hope, substantially changed by the conditions of the renewed Armistice. No one who has not seen with his or her own eyes the situation in Northern France can, it seems to me, realise its effects on the national feeling of the country. And in this third journey of mine, I have seen much more than Northern France. In a motor drive of some hundreds of miles, from Metz to Strasburg, through Nancy, Toul, St. Mihiel, Verdun, Chalons, over the ghastly battle-fields of Champagne, through Rheims, Chateau-Thierry, Vaux, to Paris, I have always had the same spectacle under my eyes, the same passion in my heart. If one tried to catch and summarise the sort of suppressed debate that was going on round one, a few weeks ago, between Allied opinion that was trying to reassure France, and the bitter feeling of France herself, it seemed to fall into something like the following dialogue:

[2] These pages were written in the first week of February.

"All is well. The Peace Conference is sitting in Paris."

"Yes—*but what about France?*"

"President Wilson and Mr. Lloyd George have gradually brought the recalcitrant elements into line. The League of Nations is a reality."

"*Yes—but what about France?* Has the President been to see these scores of ruined towns, these hundreds of wiped-out villages, these fantastic wrecks of mines and factories, these leagues on leagues of fruitful land given back to waste, these shell-blasted forests, these broken ghosts of France's noblest churches?"

"The President has made a Sunday excursion from Paris to Rheims. He saw as much as a winter day of snow and fog would allow him to see. France must be patient. Everything takes time."

"Yes!—so long as we can be sure that the true position is not only understood, but felt. But our old, rich, and beautiful country, with all the accumulations on its soil of the labour, the art, the thought of uncounted generations, has been in this war the buffer between German savagery and the rest of Europe. Just as our armies bore the first brunt and held the pass, till civilisation could rally to its own defence, so our old towns and villages have died, that our neighbours might live secure. We have suffered most in war—we claim the first thought in peace. We live in the heart and on the brink of danger. Our American Allies have a No Man's Land of the Atlantic between them and the formidable and cruel race which has wreaked this ruin, and is already beginning to show a Hydra-like power of recuperation, after its defeat; we have only a river, and not always that. We have the right to claim that our safety and restoration, the safety of the country which has suffered most, should at this moment be the first thought of Europe. You speak to us of the League of Nations?—By all means. Readjustments in the Balkans and the East?—As much as you please. But here stands the Chief Victim of the war— and to the Chief Victim belongs of right the chief and first place in men's thoughts, and in the settlement. Do not allow us even to *begin* to ask ourselves whether, after all, we have not paid too much for the alliance we gloried in?"

Some such temper as this has been showing itself since the New Year, in the discontent of the French Press, in the irritation of French talk and correspondence. And, of course, behind the bewildered and almost helpless consciousness of such a loss in accumulated wealth as no other European country has ever known before, there is the ever-burning sense of the human loss which so heavily deepens and complicates the material loss. One of the French Ministers has lately said that France has lost three millions of population, men, women, and children, through the war. The fighting operations alone have cost her over a million and a half, at least, of the best manhood of France and her Colonies. *One million and a half!* That figure had become a familiar bit of statistics to me; but it was not till I stood the other day in that vast military cemetery of Chalons, to which General Gouraud had sent me, that, to use a phrase of Keats, it was "proved" upon "one's own pulses." Seven thousand men lie buried there, their wreathed crosses standing shoulder to shoulder, all fronting one way, like a division on parade, while the simple monument that faces them utters its perpetual order of the day: "Death is nothing, so long as the Country lives. *En Avant!*"

And with that recollection goes also another, which I owe to the same General—one of the idols of the French Army!—of a little graveyard far up in the wilds of the Champagne battle-field—the "Cimetiere de Mont Muret," whence the eye takes in for miles and miles nothing but the trench-seamed hillsides and the bristling fields of wire. Here on every grave, most of them of nameless dead, collected after many months from the vast battle-field, lie heaped the last possessions of the soldier who sleeps beneath—his helmet, his haversack, his water-bottle, his *spade*. These rusty spades were to me a tragic symbol, not only of the endless, heart-wearing labour which had produced those trenched hillsides, but also of that irony of things, by which that very labour which protected the mysterious and spiritual thing which the Frenchman calls *patrie*, was at the same time ruining and sterilising the material base from which it springs—the *soil*, which the Frenchman loves with an understanding tenacity, such as perhaps inspires no other countryman in the world. In Artois and Picardy our own British graves lie thickly scattered over the murdered earth; and those of America's young and heroic dead, in the battle-fields of Soissons, the Marne, and the Argonne, have given it, this last year, a new consecration. But here in England our land is fruitful and productive, owing to the pressure of the submarine campaign, as it never was before; British farming and the American fields have cause to bless rather than to curse the war. Only in France has the tormented and poisoned earth itself been blasted by the war, and only in France, even where there are no trenches, have whole countrysides gone out of cultivation, so that in the course of a long motor drive, the sight of a solitary plough at work, or merely a strip of newly ploughed land amid the rank and endless waste, makes one's heart leap.

No!—France is quite right. Her suffering, her restoration, her future safety, as against Germany, these should be, must be, the first thought of the Allies in making peace. And it is difficult for those of us who have not seen, *to feel*, as it is politically necessary, it seems to me, we should feel.

Since I was in France, however, a fortnight ago, the proceedings in connection with the extension of the Armistice, and the new restrictions and obligations laid on Germany, have profoundly affected the situation in the direction that France desires. And when the President returns from the

United States, whither he is now bound, he will surely go—and not for a mere day or two!—to see for himself on the spot what France has suffered. If so, some deep, popular instincts in France will be at once appeased and softened, and Franco-American relations, I believe, greatly improved.

No doubt, if the President made a mistake in not going at once to the wrecked districts before the Peace Conference opened—and no one has insisted on this more strongly than American correspondents—it is clear that it was an idealist's mistake. Ruins, the President seems to have said to himself, can wait; what is essential is that the League of Nations idea, on which not Governments only, but *peoples* are hanging, should be rapidly "clothed upon" by some practical shape; otherwise the war is morally and spiritually lost.

Certainly the whole grandiose conception of the League, so vague and nebulous when the President arrived in Europe, has been marvellously brought out of the mists into some sort of solidity, during these January weeks. Not, I imagine, for some of the reasons that have been given. An able American journalist, for instance, writing to the *Times*, ascribes the advance of the League of Nations project entirely to the close support given to the President by Mr. Lloyd George and the British Government; and he explains this support as due to the British conviction "that the war has changed the whole position of Great Britain in the world. The costs of the struggle in men, in money, in *prestige* (the italics are mine), have cut very deeply; the moral effect of the submarine warfare in its later phase, and of last year's desperate campaign, have left their marks upon the Englishman, and find expression in his conduct.... British comment frankly recognises that it will never again be within the power of Great Britain, even if there were the desire, to challenge America in war or in peace."

In other words, the support given by Great Britain to President Wilson's ideas means that British statesmen are conscious of a loss of national power and prestige, and of a weakened Empire behind them.

Hasty words, I think!—and, in my belief, very wide of the mark. At any rate I may plead that during my own month in France I have been in contact with many leading men in many camps, English, French, and American, and both military and diplomatic, especially with the British Army and its chiefs; and so far from perceiving in the frankest and most critical talk of our own people—and how critical we are of our own doings those know who know us best—any sense of lost prestige or weakened power, my personal impression is overwhelmingly the other way. We are indeed anxious and willing to share responsibilities, say in Africa, and the Middle East, with America as with France. Why not? The mighty elder power is eager to see America realise her own world position, and come forward to take her share in a world-ordering, which has lain too heavy until now on England's sole shoulders. She is glad and thankful—the "weary Titan"—to hand over some of her responsibilities to America, and to share many of the rest. She wants nothing more for herself—the Great Mother of Nations—why should she? She has so much. But loss of prestige? The feeling in those with whom I have talked, is rather the feeling of Kipling's *Recessional*—a profound and wondering recognition that the Imperial bond has indeed stood so magnificently the test of these four years, just as Joseph Chamberlain, the Empire-builder, believed and hoped it would stand, when the day of testing came; a pride in what the Empire has done too deep for many words; coupled with the stubborn resolution, which says little and means every-thing—that the future shall be worthy of the past.

And as to the feeling of the Army—it is expressed, and, as far as I have been able to judge from much talk with those under his command, most truly expressed, in Field-Marshal Sir Douglas Haig's December despatch—which came out, as it happens, the very day I had the honour of standing at his side in the Commander-in-Chief's room, at G.H.Q., and looking with him at the last maps of the final campaign. "The effect of the great assaults," says the Field-Marshal, "in which, during nine days of battle (September 26th—October 5th), the First, Third, and Fourth Armies stormed the line of the Canal du

Nord, and broke through the Hindenburg line, upon the subsequent course of the campaign, was decisive.... Great as were the material losses the enemy had suffered, the effect of so overwhelming a defeat upon a *morale* already deteriorated, was of even larger importance." Again: "By the end of October, the rapid succession of heavy blows dealt by the British forces had had a cumulative effect, both moral and material, upon the German Armies. The British Armies were now in a position to force an immediate conclusion." That conclusion was forced in the battle of the Sambre (1st to 11th November). By that "great victory," says Sir Douglas Haig, "the enemy's resistance was definitely broken;" and thus "in three months of epic fighting the British Armies in France had brought to a sudden and dramatic end the great wearing-out battle of the past four years."

Do these sentences—the utterances of a man conspicuously modest and reticent in statement, indicate any consciousness of "lost prestige" in "a last desperate campaign"?

The fact is—or so it seemed to me—that while the British Army salutes with all its heart, the glorious record of that veteran Army of France which bore the brunt of the first years of war, which held the gate at Verdun at whatever cost in heroic lives, and inscribed upon its shield last year the counter-attacks in the Marne salient, and the superb stand of General Gouraud in Champagne; and while, at the same time, it realises and acknowledges to the full the enormous moral and military effect of the warm American tide, as it came rushing over France through the early summer of last year, and the gallantry of those splendid American lads, who, making mock of death, held the crossing of the Marne, took Bouresches and Belleau Wood, fought their hardest under General Mangin in the Soissons counter-attack of July 18th, and gallantly pushed their way, in spite of heavy losses, through the Argonne to the Meuse at the end of the campaign—there is yet no doubt in any British military mind that it was the British Army which brought the war to its victorious end. The British Army had grown, after the great defensive battle of the spring, by a kind

Mrs. Humphry Ward

of national rebound, of which there have been many instances in our history, to a wonderful military strength and efficiency, and to it fell, not by any choice of its own, so to speak, but by the will of the gods, and the natural disposition of events, the final and decisive strokes of the war. The French had already "saved Europe by their example," through three bloody and heroic years, and they were bound, in 1918, to economise, where possible, their remaining men; while, if the war had lasted another six months, *or* if America had come in a year earlier, the decisive battles might well have fallen to the American Army and General Pershing. But, as it happened, the British Army was at its zenith of power, numbers, and efficiency, when the last hammer-blows of the war had to be given—and our Army gave them. I do not believe there is a single instructed American or French officer who would deny this. But, if so, it is a fact which will and must make itself permanently felt in the consciousness of the Empire.

In one of the bare rooms of that Ecole Militaire, at Montreuil, where the British General Staff has worked since 1916, I saw on a snowy day at the end of January a chart covering an entire wall, which held me riveted. It was the war at a glance—so far as the British Army is concerned—from January, 1916, to the end. The rising or falling of our bayonet strength, the length of line held, casualties, prisoners—everything was there—and when finally the Hindenburg line is broken, after the great nine days of late September and early October, the prisoners' line leaps suddenly to such a height that a new piece has to be added perpendicularly to the chart, and the wall can hardly take it in. What does that leaping line mean? *Simply the collapse of the German morale*—the final and utter defeat of the German Army as a fighting force. I hope with all my heart that the General Staff will allow that chart to be published before the fickle popular memory has forgotten too much of the war.[3]

[3] By the kindness of General Sir Herbert Lawrence, Chief of the General Staff, I am able to give a small reproduction of this chart, which will be found at the end

of the book, with an explanation written by Captain W.O. Barton.

Let me then say, in recapitulation, and as presenting the main thesis of these papers, that to the British mind, at any rate, so inarticulate often, yet so tenacious, the Western campaign of last year presents itself as having been fought by three national Armies:

(1) The veteran and glorious French Army, which, while providing in Marshal Foch the master-spirit of the last unified effort, was yet, after its huge sacrifices at Verdun, in Champagne, and many another stricken field, inevitably husbanding its resources in men, and yielding to the Armies of its Allies the hottest work in the final struggle;

(2) The British Army, which, after its victorious reaction from its March defensive, was at the very height of its four years' development in men, training, and *morale*, and had already shown by the stand of the Third Army at Arras, at the very fiercest moment of the German onslaught, that although Germany might still attack, it was now certain that, so long as the British Army was in the field, she could not win the war: and finally;

(3) The young and growing American Army, which had only been some six months in the fighting line, and was still rather a huge *promise*, though of capital importance, both politically and militarily, than a performance. It was brave and ardent, like a young eaglet, "with eyes intentive to bedare the sun;" but it had its traditions to lay down, its experience to buy, and large sections of its military lesson still to learn. It could not, as a fighting force, have determined the war last year; and the war was finally won, under the supreme command of a great Frenchman, by the British Army, acting in concert with the French and American armies—and supported by the British naval blockade, and the British, French, and Serbian military successes in the East.

In such a summary I am, naturally, merely a *porte-voix*, trying to reproduce the thoughts of many minds, as I came across them in France. But if this is the general upshot of the situation, and the general settled conviction of the instructed British mind, as I believe it to be, our alliance with France and our friendship with America, so passionately upheld by all that is best in our respective nations, have both of them nothing to lose from its temperate statement. Great Britain, in spite of our national habit of running ourselves down, is not, indeed, supporting the League of Nations from any sense at all of lost prestige or weakened power, but from an idealism no less hopeful and insistent than that of America, coupled with a loathing of war no less strong.

The League of Nations!—A year ago how many of us had given any serious thought to what was then a phrase, a dream, on which in the dark days of last spring it seemed a mere waste of time to dwell? And yet, week by week, since the New Year began, the dream has been slowly taking to itself body and form.

On the very day (January 25th) when the League of Nations resolution was passed at the Paris Conference, I happened to spend an interesting hour in President Wilson's company, at the Villa Murat. Mrs. Wilson, whose gentle kindness and courtesy were very widely appreciated in Paris, had asked me to come in at six o'clock, and await the President's return from the Conference. I found her with five or six visitors round her, members of the Murat family, come to pay a visit to the illustrious guest to whom they had lent their house—the Princesse Murat, talking fluent English, her son in uniform, her widowed daughter and two delicious little children. In little more than five minutes, the President came in, and the beautiful room made a rich setting for an interesting scene. He entered, radiant, and with his first words, standing in our midst, told us that the Conference had just passed the League of Nations resolution. The two tiny children approached him, the little girl curtseyed to him, the little boy kissed his hand; and then they vanished, to remember, perhaps, fifty years hence, the dim figure of a tall and smiling man, whom they saw on a day marked in history.

The President took his seat as the centre of our small circle. I am not going to betray the confidence of what was a private visit, but general impressions are not, I think, forbidden. I still seem to see the Princesse Murat opposite me, in black, her fingers playing with her pearls as she talked; the French officer with folded arms beside her; next to him the young widowed lady, whose name I did not catch, then Mrs. Wilson, with the intelligent face of her secretary, Miss Benham, in the background, and between myself and Princesse Murat, the easy, attractive presence of the man whom this old Europe, with one accord, is now discussing, criticising, blaming or applauding. The President talked with perfect simplicity and great apparent frankness. There is a curious mingling in his face, it seemed to me, of something formidable, at times almost threatening, with charm and sweetness. You are in the presence of something held in leash; that something is clearly a will of remarkable quality and power. You are also in the presence of something else, not less strongly controlled, a consciousness of success, which is in itself a promise of further success. The manner has in it nothing of the dictator, and nothing of the pedant; but in the President's instinctive and accomplished choice of words and phrases, something reminded me of the talk of George Eliot as I heard it fifty years ago; of the account also given me quite recently by an old friend and classmate of the President, describing the remarkable pains taken with him as a boy, by his father, to give him an unfailing command of correct and musical English.

The extraordinary effectiveness lent by this ease and variety of diction to a man who possesses not only words but ideas, is strongly realised in Paris, where an ideal interpreter, M. Paul Mantoux, is always at hand to put whatever the President says into perfect French. M. Jusserand had given me an enthusiastic account, a few days before this little gathering at the Villa Murat, of an impromptu speech at a luncheon given to the President by the Senate, and in listening to the President's conversation, I understood what M. Jusserand had felt, and what a weapon at need—(how rare also among public men!)—is this skilled excellence in expression, which the President commands, and commands above all, so some of his shrewdest observers tell me, when he is thrown suddenly on his own resources, has no scrap of paper to help him, and must speak as Nature and the Fates bid him. It is said that the irreverent American Army, made a little restive during the last months of the year by the number of Presidential utterances it was expected to read, and impatient to get to the Rhine, was settling down in the weeks before the Armistice, with a half-sulky resignation to "another literary winter." One laughs, but never were the art and practice of literature more signally justified as a power among men than by this former Professor and Head of a college, who is now among the leading political forces of the world.

Well, we talked of many things—of the future local habitation of the League of Nations, of the Russian *impasse*, and the prospects of Prinkipo, of Mr. Lloyd George's speech that day at the Conference, of Siberia and Japan, of Ireland even! There was no difficulty anywhere; no apparent concealment of views and opinions. But there was also no carelessness and no indiscretion. I came away feeling that I had seen a remarkable man, on one of the red-letter days of his life; revolving, too, an old Greek tag which had become familiar to me:

"Mortal men grow wise by seeing. But without seeing, how can any man foretell the future—how he may fare?"

In other words, call no work happy till it is accomplished. Yes!—but men and women are no mere idle spectators of a destiny imposed on them, as the Greeks sometimes, but only sometimes, believed. They themselves *make* the future. If Europe wants the League of Nations, and the end of war, each one of us must turn to, *and work*, each in our own way. Since the day of the first Conference resolution, the great scheme, like some veiled Alcestis, has come a good deal further down the stage of the world. There it stands while we debate; as

Thanatos and Heracles fought over the veiled queen. But in truth it rests with us, the audience, and not with any of the leading characters in the drama, to bring that still veiled figure into life and light, and to give it a lasting place in the world's household.

Meanwhile the idea is born; but into a Europe still ringing with the discords of war, and in a France still doubtful and full of fears. There is a brooding and threatening presence beyond the Rhine. And among the soldiers going and coming between the Rhine bridge-heads and Paris, there is a corresponding and anxious sense of the fierce vitality of Germany, and of the absence of any real change of heart among her people. Meanwhile the relations between Great Britain and America were never closer, and the determination of the leading men in both countries to forge a bond beyond breaking between us was never so clear. There are problems and difficulties ahead in this friendship, as in all friendships, whether national or individual. But a common good-will will solve them, a common resolve to look the facts of the moment and the hopes of the future steadily in the face.

Mrs. Humphry Ward

CHAPTER II

THE DEFENSIVE BATTLE OF LAST SPRING

I.

March, 1919.

Among the impressions and experiences of my month in France there are naturally some that stand out in particularly high relief. I have just described one of them. But I look back to others not less vivid—an evening, for instance, with General Horne and his staff; a walk along the Hindenburg line and the Canal du Nord, north and south of the Arras-Bapaume road; dinner with General Gouraud in the great building at Strasbourg, which was formerly the headquarters of the German Army Corps holding Alsace, and is now the French Prefecture; the eastern battle-field at Verdun, and that small famous room under the citadel, through which all the leaders of the war have passed; Rheims Cathedral emerging ghostly from the fog, with, in front of it, a group of motor-cars and two men shaking hands, the British Premier and the Cardinal-Archbishop; that desolate heart of the Champagne battle-field, where General Gouraud, with the American Army on his right, made his September push towards Vouziers and Mezieres; General Pershing in his office, and General Pershing *en petit comite* in a friend's drawing-room, in both settings the same attractive figure, with the same sudden half-mischievous smile and the same observant eyes; and, finally, that rabbit-warren of small, barely furnished rooms in the old Ecole

Militaire at Montreuil, where the British General Staff worked during the war, when it was not moving in its staff train up and down behind the front.

But I do not intend to make these letters a mere *omnium gatherum* of recollections. All through, my object has been to lay hold of the main outline of what has happened on the Western front during the past eleven months, and if I could, to make them clear to other civilians, men and women, as clearly and rapidly as possible, in this interval between the regime of *communiques* and war-correspondence under which we have lived so long, and those detailed and scientific histories which every Army, and probably every corps and division, is now either writing, or preparing to write, about its own doings in the war. Meanwhile the official reports drawn up by each Army under the British Command are "secret documents." The artillery dispositions of the great battles which brought the war to an end cannot yet be disclosed. There can, therefore, be no proper maps of these battles for some time to come, while some of the latest developments in offensive warfare which were to have been launched upon the enemy had the war continued, are naturally not for the public for a good while ahead. And considering that, year by year, we are still discussing and investigating the battles of a hundred years ago—(look for instance at the lists of recent books on the Napoleonic campaigns in the Cambridge Moddern History!)—we may guess at the time mankind will take hereafter in writing about and elucidating a war, where in many of the great actions, as a Staff Officer remarked to me, a Waterloo might have been lost without being missed, or won without being more than a favourable incident in an otherwise perhaps unfavourable whole.

At the same time, this generation has got somehow—as an ingredient in its daily life—to form as clear a mental picture as it can of the war as a whole, and especially just now of its closing months in France. For the history of those last months is at the present moment an *active agent in the European situation*. What one may call the war-consciousness of France, with the first battle of the Marne, glorious Verdun, the Champagne battle-field, the victorious leadership of Marshal Foch, on the one hand—her hideous losses in men, her incalculable loss in material and stored-up wealth, and her stern claim for adequate protection in future, on the other, as its main elements; the war-consciousness of Great Britain and the Empire, turning essentially on the immortal defence of the Ypres salient and the Channel ports, the huge sacrifices of the Somme, the successes and disappointments of 1917, the great defensive battle of last March, and the immediate and brilliant reaction, leading in less than five months to the beginning of that series of great actions on the British front which finished the war—all interpenetrated with the sense of perpetual growth in efficiency and power; and finally, the American war-consciousness, as it emerged from the war, with its crusading impulse intact, its sense of boundless resources, and its ever-fresh astonishment at the irrevocable part America was now called on to play in European affairs:—amid these three great and sometimes clashing currents, the visitor to France lived and moved in the early weeks of the year. And then, of course, there was the Belgian war-consciousness—a new thing for Belgium and for Europe. But with that I was not concerned.

Let me try to show by an illustration or two drawn from my own recent experience what the British war-consciousness means.

It was a beautiful January day when we started from the little inn at Cassel for Ypres, Menin, Lille, Lens, and Vimy. From the wonderful window at the back of the inn, high perched as Cassel is above a wide plain, one looked back upon the roads to St. Omer and the south, and thought of the days last April, when squadron after squadron of French cavalry came riding hot and fast along them to the relief of our hard-pressed troops, after the break of the Portuguese sector of the line at Richebourg St. Vaast. But our way lay north, not south, through a district that seemed strangely familiar to me, though in fact I had only passed forty-eight hours in it, in 1916. Forty-eight hours, however, in the war-zone, at a time of active fighting, and that long before any other person of my sex had been allowed to approach the actual firing-line on the British front, were not like other hours; and, perhaps, from much thinking of them, the Salient and the approaches to it, as I saw them in 1916 from the Scherpenberg hill, had become a constant image in the mind. Only, instead of seeing Ypres from the shelter of the Scherpenberg Windmill, as a distant phantom in the horizon mists, beyond the shell-bursts in the battle-field below us, we were now to go through Ypres itself, then wholly forbidden ground, and out beyond it into some of the ever-famous battle-fields that lie north and south of the Ypres-Menin road.

One hears much talk in Paris of the multitudes who will come to see the great scenes of the war, as soon as peace is signed, when the railways are in a better state, and the food problems less, if not solved. The multitudes indeed have every right to come, for it is nations, not standing armies, that have won this war. But, personally, one may be glad to have seen these sacred places again, during this intermediate period of utter solitude and desolation, when their very loneliness "makes deep silence in the heart—for thought to do its part." The roads in January were clear, and the Army gone. The only visitors were a few military cars, and men of the salvage corps, directing German prisoners in the gathering up of live shells and hand-grenades, of tons of barbed wire and trip wire, and all the other *debris* of battle that still lie thick upon the ground. In a few months perhaps there will be official guides conducting parties through the ruins, and in a year or two, the ruins of Ypres themselves may have given place to the rising streets of a new city. As they now are, a strange and sinister majesty surrounds them. At the entrance to the town there still hangs the notice: "Troops are not to enter Ypres except on special duty"; and the grass-grown heaps of masonry are labelled: "It is dangerous to dig among these ruins." But there was no one digging when we were there—no one moving, except ourselves. Ypres seemed to me beyond recovery as a town, just as Lens is; but whereas Lens is just a shapeless ugliness which men will clear away rejoicing as soon as their energies are free for rebuilding, Ypres in ruin has still beauty enough and dignity enough to serve—with the citadel at Verdun—as the twin symbol of the war. There was a cloud of jackdaws circling round the great gashed tower where the inner handiwork of the fifteenth-century builders lay open to sky and sun. I watched them against the blue, gathering in, also, the few details of lovely work that still remain here and there on the face of what was once the splendid Cloth Hall, the glory of these border lands. And one tried to imagine how men and women would stand there a hundred years hence, amid what developments of this strange new world that the war has brought upon us, and with what thoughts.

Beyond, we were in the wide, shell-pocked waste of the huge battle-field, with many signs on its scarred face of the latest fighting of all, the flooding back of the German tide in last April over these places which it had cost us our best lives to gain, and of the final victorious advance of King Albert and the British Second Army which sent the Germans flying back through Limburg to their own land. Beside us, the innumerable, water-logged shell-holes, in which, at one time or another in the swaying forward and backward of the fight, the lives of brave men have been so piteously lost, strangled in mud and ooze; here a mere sign-post which tells you where Hooge stood; there the stumps that mark Sanctuary Wood and Polygon Wood, and another sign-post which bears the ever-famous name of Gheluvelt. In the south-eastern distance rises the spire of Menin church. And this is *the Menin Road.* How it haunted the war news for months and years, like a blood-stained presence! While to the south-east, I make out Kemmel, Scherpenberg, and the Mont des Cats and in the far north-west a faint line with a few trees on it—*Passchendaele!*

Passchendaele!—name of sorrow and of glory. What were the British losses, in that three months' fighting from June to November, 1917, which has been called the "Third Battle of Ypres," which began with the victory of the Messines ridge and culminated in the Canadian capture of Passchendaele?[4] Outside the inner circle of those who know, there are many figures given. They are alike only in this that they seem to grow perpetually. Heroic, heart-breaking wrestle with the old hostile forces of earth and water—black earth and creeping water and strangling mud! We won the ridge and we held it till the German advance in April last forced our temporary withdrawal; we had pushed the Germans off the high ground into the marsh lands beyond; but we failed, as everyone knows, in the real strategic objects of the attack, and the losses in the autumn advance on Passchendaele were an important and untoward factor in the spring fighting of 1918.

[4] Mr. Bonar Law has stated in the House of Commons since these lines were written that the losses in the third battle of Ypres, from Messines to Passchendaele, July—October, 1917, were 228,000.

How deeply this Ypres salient enters into the war-consciousness of Britain and the Empire! As I stand looking over the black stretches of riddled earth, at the half-demolished pill-boxes in front, at the muddy pools in the shell-holes under a now darkening sky; at the flat stretches between us and Kemmel where lie Zillebeke and St. Eloi, and a score of other names which will be in the mouth of history hundreds of years hence, no less certainly than the names of those little villages north and south of Thermopylae, which saw the advance of the Persians and the vigil of the Greeks—a confusion of things read and heard, rush through one's mind, taking new form and vividness from this actual scene in which they happened. There, at those cross roads, broke the charge of the Worcesters, on that most critical day of all in the First Battle of Ypres, when the fate of the Allies hung on a thread, and this "homely English regiment," with its famous record in the Peninsula and elsewhere, drove back the German advance and saved the line. I turn a little to the south and I am looking towards Klein Zillebeke where the Household Cavalry charged, and Major Hugh Dawnay at their head "saved the British position," and lost his own gallant life. Straight ahead of us, down the Menin road towards Gheluvelt, came the Prussian Guards, the Emperor's own troops with their master's eye on them, on November 11th, when the First Division in General Haig's

First Corps, checked them, enfiladed them, mowed them down, till the flower of the Imperial troops fell back in defeat, never knowing by how small a fraction they had missed victory, how thin a line had held them, how little stood between them and the ports that fed the British Army. Here on these flats to my right were Lord Cavan's Guards, and on either side of him General Allenby's cavalry, and General Byng's; while, if one turns to the north towards the distance which hides Sonnebeke and Bixschoote, one is looking over the ground so magnificently held on our extreme left by General Dubois and his 9th French Corps.

Guards, Yorkshires, Lancashires, London Scottish, Worcesters, Royal Scots Fusiliers, Highlanders, Gordons, Leicesters—all the familiar names of the old Army are likend with this great story. It was an English and Scotch victory, the victory of these Islands, won before the "rally of the Empire" had time to develop, before a single Canadian or Australian soldier had landed in France.

But that is only the first, though in some ways the greatest, chapter in this bloodstained book. Memory runs on nearly six months, and we come to that awful April afternoon, when the French line broke under the first German gas attack, and the Canadians on their right held on through two days and nights, gassed and shelled, suffering frightful casualties, but never yielding, till the line was safe, and fresh troops had come up. It was not six weeks since at Neuve Chapelle the Canadians had for the first time, while not called on to take much active part themselves, seen the realities of European battle; and the cheers of the British troops at Ypres as the exhausted Dominion troops came back from the trenches will live in history.

Messines, and the victory of June, 1917—Passchendaele, and the losses of that grim winter—all the points indeed of this dim horizon from north-west to south-east have their imperishable meaning for Great Britain and the Dominions. For quite apart from the main actions which stand out, fighting and death never ceased in the Ypres salient.

Then, as the great Army of the gallant dead seemed to gather round one on this famous road, and over these shell-torn flats, a sudden recollection of a letter which I received in August, 1918, brought a tightening of the throat. A Canadian lady, writing from an American camp in the east of France, appealed to myself and other writers to do something to bring home to the popular mind of America a truer knowledge of what the British Armies had done in the war. "I see here," says the writer, "hundreds of the finest remaining white men on earth every week. They are wonderful military material, and very attractive and lovable boys. But it discourages all one's hope for the future unity and friendship between us all to realise as I have done the last few months that the majority of these men are entering the fight, firmly believing that 'England has not done her share—that France had done it all—the Colonials have done all the hard fighting, etc.'" And she proceeds to attribute the state of things to the "belittling reports" of England's share in the war given in the newspapers which reach these "splendid men" from home.

A similar statement has come to me within the last few days, in another letter from an English lady in an American camp near Verdun, who speaks of the tragic ignorance—for tragic it is when one thinks of all that depends on Anglo-American understanding in the future!—shown by the young Americans in the camp where she is at work, of the share of Great Britain in the war.

Alack! How can we bring our two nations closer together in this vital matter? Of course there is no belittlement of the British part in the war among those Americans who have been brought into any close contact with it. And in my small efforts to meet the state of things described in the letters I have quoted, some of the warmest and most practical sympathy shown has come from Americans. But in the vast population of the United States with its mixed elements, some of them inevitably hostile to this country, how easy for the currents of information and opinion to go astray over large tracts of country at any rate, and at the suggestion of an

Mrs. Humphry Ward

anti-British press!

The only effective remedy, it seems to me, would be the remedy of eyes and ears! Would it not be well, before the whole of the great American Army goes home, that as many as possible of those still in France—groups, say, of non-commissioned officers from various American divisions, representing both the older and the newer levies, and drawn from different local areas—should be given the opportunity of seeing and studying the older scenes of the war on the British front?—and that our own men, also, should be able to see for themselves, not only the scenes of the American fighting of last year, but the vast preparations of all kinds that America was building up in France for the further war that might have been; preparations which, as no one doubts, changed the whole atmosphere of the struggle?

"England has not done her share!"

How many thousands of British dead—men from every county in England and Scotland, from loyal Ireland, from every British dominion and colony—lie within the circuit of these blood-stained hills of Ypres? How many more in the Somme graveyards?—round Lens and Arras and Vimy?—about Bourlon Wood and Cambrai?—or in the final track of our victorious Armies breaking through the Hindenburg line on their way to Mons? Gloriously indeed have the Dominions played their part in this war; but of all the casualties suffered by the Armies of the Empire, 80 *per cent* of them fell on the population of these islands. America was in the great struggle for a year and a half, and in the real fightingline for about six months. She has lost some 54,000 of her gallant sons; and we sorrow for them with her.

But through four long years scarcely a family in Great Britain and the Dominions that possessed men on the fighting fronts—and none were finally exempt except on medical or industrial grounds—but was either in mourning for, or in constant fear of death for one or more of its male members, whether by bullet, shell-fire or bomb, or must witness the return to them of husbands, brothers, and sons, more or less injured for life. The total American casualties are 264,000. The total British casualties—among them from 700,000 to 800,000 dead—are 2,228,000 out of a total white population for the Empire of not much more than two-thirds of the population of the United States. There is small room for "belittling" here. A silent clasp of the hands between our two nations would seem to be the natural gesture in face of such facts as these.

II.

Such thoughts, however, belong to the emotional or tragic elements in the British war-consciousness. Let me turn to others of a different kind—the intellectual and reflective elements—and the changing estimates which they bring about.

Take for instance what we have been accustomed to call the "March retreat" of last year. The dispatch of Sir Douglas Haig describing the actions of March and April last year was so headed in the *Times*, though nothing of the kind appears in the official publication. And we can all remember in England the gnawing anxiety of every day and every hour from March 21st up to the end of April, when the German offensive had beaten itself out, on the British front at least, and the rushing over of the British reinforcements, together with the rapid incoming of the Americans, had given the British Army the breathing space of which three months later it made the use we know.

"But why," asks one of the men best qualified to speak in our Army—"why use the words 'retreat' and 'disaster' at all?" They were indeed commonly used at the time both in England and abroad, and have been often used since about the fighting of the British Army last March and April. Strictly speaking, my interlocutor suggests, neither word is applicable. The British Army indeed fell back some thirty-five miles on its southern front, till the German attack was finally stayed before Amiens. The British centre stood firm from Arras to Bethune. But in the north we had to yield almost all the ground gained in the Salient the year before, and some that had never yet been in German hands. We lost heavily in men and guns, and a shudder of alarm ran through all the Allied countries.

Nevertheless what Europe was then witnessing—I am of course quoting not any opinion of my own, to which I have no right, but what I have gathered from those responsible men who were in the forefront of the fighting—was in truth *a great defensive battle*, long and anxiously foreseen, in which the

German forces were double the British forces opposed to them (64 to 32 divisions—73 to 32—and so on), while none the less all that was vitally necessary to the Allied cause was finally achieved by the British Army, against these huge odds. Germany, in fact, made her last desperate effort a year ago to break through the beleaguering British, forces, and failed. On our side there was no real surprise, though our withdrawal was deeper and our losses greater than had been foreseen. The troops themselves may have been confident; it is the habit of gallant men. But the British command knew well what it had to face, and had considered carefully weeks beforehand where ground could be given—as in all probability it would have to be given—with the least disadvantage. Some accidents, if one may call them so, indeed there were—the thick white fog, for instance, which "on the morning of March 21st enveloped our outpost line, and made it impossible to see more than fifty yards in any direction, so that the machine guns and forward field-guns which had been disposed so as to cover this zone with their fire were robbed almost entirely of their effect—and the masses of German infantry advanced comparatively unharassed, so closely supporting each other that loss of direction was impossible." Hence the rapidity of the German advance through the front lines on March 21st, and the alarming break-through south of St. Quentin, where our recently extended line was weakest and newest. A second accident was the drying up of the Oise Marshes at a time when in a normal year they might have been reckoned on to stop the enemy's advance. A third piece of ill-luck was the fact that in the newest section of the British line, where the enemy attack broke at its hottest, there had been no time, since it had been given over to us by the French—who had held it lightly, as a quiet sector, during the winter—to strengthen its defences, and to do the endless digging, the railway construction, and the repair of roads, which might have made a very great difference. And, finally, there was the most dangerous accident of all—the break through of the Portuguese line at Richebourg St. Vaast, just as the tired division holding it was about to be relieved. Of that accident, as we all remember, the enemy, hungry for the Channel ports, made his very worst and most; till the French and British fought him to a final stand before Hazebrouck and Ypres.

Meanwhile, the strategic insight of Marshal Foch, who assumed complete control of the Allied Armies in France and Belgium on March 26th, combined with the experienced and cool-headed leadership of the British Commander-in-Chief, refused to dissipate the French reserves, so important to the future course of the war, in any small or piecemeal reinforcement of the British lines. The risks of the great moment had to be taken, and both the French and British Commanders had complete faith in the capacity of the British Army to meet them. And when all is said, when our grave losses in casualties, prisoners, and guns are fully admitted, what was the general result? The Germans had failed to gain either of their real objectives:—either the Channel ports, or the division of the British Armies from the French. They wore themselves out against a line which recoiled indeed but never broke, and was all the time filling up and strengthening from behind. The losses inflicted on their immense reserves reacted on all the subsequent fighting of the year, both on the Aisne and the Marne. And when the British Armies had brought the huge attack to a standstill—which for the centre and south of our line had been already attained ten days after the storm broke—and knew the worst that had happened or could happen to them; when the Australians had recaptured Villers-Bretonneux; when the weeks passed and the offensive ceased; when all gaps in our ranks were filled by the rush of reinforcements from home, and the American Army poured steadily across the Atlantic, the tension and peril of the spring passed steadily into the confident strength and—expectation of the summer. The British Army had held against an attack which could never be repeated, and the future was with the Allies.

Let us remember that at no time in our fighting withdrawal, either on the Somme or on the Lys, was there "anything approaching a break-down of command, or a failure in morale." So the Field Marshal. On the other hand, all over the vast battle-field—in every part of the hard "waiting game" which for a time the British Armies were called to play, men did the most impossible and heroic things. Gun detachments held their posts till every man was killed or wounded; infantry who had neither rest nor sleep for days together, fought "back to back in the trenches, shooting both to front and rear." Occasional confusion, even local panic, occasional loss of communication and misunderstanding of orders, occasional incompetence and stupidity there must be in such a vast backward sweep of battle, but skill, purpose, superb bravery were never lacking in any portion of the field; and the German *communiques* exultantly announcing the "total defeat of the British Armies" may be compared, *mutatis mutandis*, with the reports from German Headquarters just before the first battle of the Marne.

"The defeat of the English is complete," said the German High Command in the latter days of August, 1914. "The English Army is retreating in the most complete disorder.... The British have been completely defeated to the north of St. Quentin"—and so on. And yet a week later, as General Maurice, with much fresh evidence, has lately shown, the Army thus disposed of on paper had rejoicingly turned upon von Kluck, and was playing a vital part in the great victory of the Marne. So last spring, the losses and withdrawals of a vaster defensive action, coupled with the stubborn and tenacious hold of the British Army, last March and April, were the inevitable and heroic prelude to the victorious recoil of August, and the final battles of the war. Inevitable, because no forethought or exertion on the British side could have averted the German onslaught, determined as it was by the breakdown of the whole Eastern front of the war, and the letting loose upon the Western front of immense forces previously held by the Russian armies. These forces, after the Russian *debacle*, were released against us, week by week, till in March the balance of numbers, which was almost even in January, had risen on the German side to a superiority of 150,000 bayonets! The dispatch of divisions to Italy; the recall of men to the shipyards and the mines to meet the submarine danger; the heavy fighting in the Salient and at Cambrai in the latter half of 1917; the lack of time for training new levies, owing to our depleted line and reserves:—all these causes contributed to sharpen the peril in which England stood.[5] But it is in such straits as these that our race shows its quality.

[5] See the Chart at end of Book.

And in this fighting, for the first time in British history, and in the history of Europe, Americans stood side by side in battle with British and French. "In the battle of March and April," says Sir Douglas Haig, "American and British troops have fought shoulder to shoulder in the same trenches, and have shared together in the satisfaction of beating off German attacks. All ranks of the British Army look forward to the day when the rapidly growing strength of the American Army will allow American and British soldiers *to co-operate in offensive action.*"

That day came without much delay. It carried the British Army to Mons, and the young American Army to Sedan.

* * * * *

Looking out from the Vimy Ridge six weeks ago, and driving thence through Arras across the Drocourt-Queant line to Douai and Valenciennes, I was in the very heart of that triumphant stand of the Third and First Armies round Arras which really determined the fate of the German attack.

The Vimy Ridge from the west is a stiffish climb. On the east also it drops steeply above Petit Vimy and Vimy, while on the south and south-east it rises so imperceptibly from the Arras road that the legend which describes the Commander-in-Chief, approaching it from that side, as asking of the officers assembled to meet him after the victory—"And where is this ridge that you say you have taken?" seems almost a reasonable tale. But to east and west there is no doubt about it. One climbs up the side overlooking Ablain St. Nazaire through shell-holes and blurred trenches, over snags of wire, and round the edges of craters, till on the top one takes breath on the wide plateau where stands the Canadian monument to those who fell in the glorious fight of April 9th, 1917, and whence the eye sweeps that wide northern and eastern plain, towards Lille on the one side and Douai on the other, which to our war-beaten and weary soldiers, looking out upon it when the ridge at last was theirs, was almost as new and strange a world as the Pacific was to its first European beholders.

Westwards across the valley whence our troops stormed the hill, rises the Bouvigny Wood, and the long, blood-stained ridge of Notre Dame de Lorette, where I stood just before the battle, in 1917. To the north we are looking through the horizon shadows to La Bassee, Bailleul, and the Salient. Immediately below the hill, in the same direction, lie the ruin heaps of Lens, and of the mining towns surrounding it; while behind us the ground slopes south and south-east to Arras and the Scarpe.

It is a tremendous position. That even the merest outsider can see. In old days the hill must have been a pleasant rambling ground for the tired workers of the coal-mining districts. Then the war-blast at its fiercest passed over it. To-day in its renewed solitude, its sacred peace, it represents one of the master points of the war, bought and held by a sacrifice of life and youth, the thought of which holds one's heart in grip, as one stands there, trying to gather in the meaning of the scene. Not one short year ago it was in the very centre of the struggle. If Arras and Vimy had not held, things would have been grave indeed. Had they been captured, says the official report of the Third Army, "our main lateral communications—Amiens—Doullens—St. Pol—St. Omer—would have been seriously threatened if not cut." The Germans were determined to have them, and they fought for them with a desperate courage. Three assault divisions were to have carried the Vimy Ridge, while other divisions were to have captured Arras and the line of the Scarpe. The attack was carried out with the greatest fierceness, men marching shoulder to shoulder into the furnace of battle.

But this time there was no fog to shield them, or to blind the British guns. The enemy losses were appalling, and after one day's fighting, in spite of the more northerly attacks on our line still to come, the German hopes of *victory* were in the dust, and—as we now know—for ever.

That is what Vimy means—what Arras means—in the fighting of last year. We ponder it as we drive through the wrecked beauty of Arras and out on to the Douai road on our way to Valenciennes. We passed slowly along the road to the east of Arras, honeycombed still with dug-outs, and gun emplacements, and past trenches and wire fields, till suddenly a mere sign-board, nothing more—"Gavrelle!"—shows us that we are approaching the famous Drocourt-Queant switch of the Hindenburg line, which the Canadians and the 17th British Corps, under Sir Henry Horne, stormed and took in September of last year. Presently, on either side of the road as we drive slowly eastward, a wilderness of trenches runs north and south. With what confident hope the Germans dug and fortified and elaborated them years ago!—with what contempt of death and danger our men carried them not six months since! And now not a sign of life anywhere—nothing but groups of white crosses here and there, emerging from the falling dusk, and the *debris* of battle along the road.

A weary way to Douai, over the worst road we have struck yet, and a weary way beyond it to Denain and Valenciennes. Darkness falls and hides the monotonous scene of ruin, which indeed begins to change as we approach Valenciennes, the Headquarters of the First Army. And at last, a bright fire in an old room piled with books and papers, a kind welcoming from the officer reigning over it, and the pleasant careworn face of an elderly lady with whom we are billeted.

Best of all, a message from the Army Commander, Sir Henry Horne, with whom we had made friends in 1917, just before the capture of the Vimy Ridge, in which the First Army played so brilliant a part.

We hastily change our travel gear, a car comes for us, and soon we find ourselves at the General's table in the midst of an easy flow of pleasant talk.

What is it that makes the special charm of the distinguished soldier, as compared with other distinguished men?

Simplicity, I suppose, and truth. The realities of war leave small room for any kind of pose. A high degree, also, of personal stoicism easily felt but not obtruded; and towards weak and small things—women and children—a natural softness and tenderness of feeling, as though a man who has upon him such stern responsibilities of life and death must needs grasp at their opposites, when and how he can; keen intelligence, *bien entendu*, modesty, courtesy; a habit of brevity; a boy's love of fun: with some such list of characteristics I find myself trying to answer my own question. They are at least conspicuous in many leaders of the Allied Armies.

"Why don't you *boom* your Generals?" said an American diplomatist to me some eight months ago. "Your public at home knows far too little about them individually. But the personal popularity of the military leader in such a national war as this is a military asset."

I believe I entirely agree with the speaker! But it is not the British military way, and the unwritten laws of the Service stand firm. So let me only remind you that General Horne led the artillery at Mons; that he has commanded the First Army since September, 1916; that, in conjunction with Sir Julian Byng, he carried the Vimy Ridge in 1917, and held the left at Arras in 1918; and, finally, that he was the northernmost of the three Army Commanders who stormed the Hindenburg line last September.

It was in his study and listening to the explanations he gave me, so clearly and kindly, of the Staff maps that lay before us, that I first realised with anything like sufficient sharpness the meaning of those words we have all repeated so often without understanding them—*"the capture of the Hindenburg line."*

What was the Hindenburg line?

CHAPTER III

TANKS AND THE HINDENBURG LINE

We left Valenciennes on the morning of January 12th. By great luck, an officer from the First Army, who knew every inch of the ground to be traversed, was with us, in addition to the officer from G.H.Q., who, as is always the case with Army visitors, accompanied us most courteously and efficiently throughout. Captain X took us by a by-road through the district south of Valenciennes, where in October last year our troops were fighting a war of movement, in open country, on two fronts—to the north and to the east. There were no trenches in the desolate fields we passed through, but many shell-holes, and the banks of every road were honeycombed with shelters, dug-outs and gun-emplacements, rough defences that as the German Army retreated our men had taken over and altered to their own needs; while to the west lay the valley of the Sensee with its marshes, the scene of some of the most critical fighting of the war.

From the wrecked centre of Cambrai a short run over field roads takes you to the high ground north-west of the city which witnessed some of the fiercest fighting of last autumn. I still see the jagged ruins of the little village of Abancourt—totally destroyed in two days' bombardment—standing sharp against the sky, on a ridge which looks over the Sensee valley; the shell-broken road in which the car—most complaisant of cars and most skilful of drivers!—finally stuck; and those hastily dug shelters on the road-side in one of which I suddenly noticed a soldier's coat and water-bottle lying just as they had been left two months before. There were no terrible sights now in these lonely fields as there were then, but occasionally, as with this coat, the refuse of battle took one back to the living presences that once filled these roads—the *men*, to whom Marshal Haig expresses the gratitude of a great Commander in many a simple yet moving passage of his last dispatch.

And every step beyond Cambrai, desolate as it is, is thronged with these invisible legions. There to our right rises the long line of Bourlon Wood—here are the sand-pits at its foot—and there are the ruined fragments of Fontaine-notre-Dame. There rushes over one again the exultation and the bitter recoil of those London days in November, 1917, when the news of the Cambrai battle came in; the glorious surprise of the tanks; the triumphant progress of Sir Julian Byng; the evening papers with their telegrams, and those tragic joy-bells that began to ring; and then the flowing back of the German wave; the British withdrawal from that high wood yonder which had cost so much to win, and from much else; the bewilderment and disappointment at home. A tired Army, and an attack pushed too far?—is that the summing up of the first battle of Cambrai? A sudden gleam had shone on that dark autumn which had seen the bitter victory and the appalling losses of Passchendaele, and then the gleam vanished, and the winter closed in, and there was nothing for the British Army but to turn its steady mind to the Russian break-down and to the ever-growing certainty of a German attack, fiercer and more formidable than had ever yet broken on the Allies.

Bourlon Wood—famous name!—fades behind us. A few rubbish heaps beside the road tell of former farms and factories. The car descends a long slope, and then, suddenly, before us runs the great dry trough of the Canal du Nord; in front, a ruined bridge, with a temporary one beside it, a ruined lock on the left, and rising ground beyond. We cross the bridge, mount a short way on the western slope, then in the darkening afternoon we walk along the front trench of the

Hindenburg line, north and south of the road—a superb trench, the finest I have yet seen, dug right down into the rock, with concrete headquarters, dressing and signal stations, machine-gun emplacements and observation posts; and, in front of it, great fields of wire, through which wide lanes have been flattened down. Now we have turned eastward, and we stand and gaze towards Cambrai, over the road we have come. The huge trench is before us, the waterless canal with its steep banks lies beyond, and on the further hill-side, trench beyond trench, as far as the eye can see, the lines still fairly clear, though in some places broken up and confused by bombardment. The officer beside me draws my attention to some marks on the ground near me—the track marks of two tanks as plain almost as when they were made. One of them, after flattening a wide passage through the wire fields for the advance of the infantry, had clambered across the trench. At our feet were the grooved marks of the descent, and we could follow them through the incredible rise on the further side; after which the protected monster—of much lighter build, however, than his predecessors on the Somme—seemed to have run north and south along the trench, silencing the deadly patter of the machine guns; while its fellow on the west side, according to its tracks at least, had also turned south, for the same purpose.

The Hindenburg line!—and the two tanks! The combination, indeed, suggests the whole story of that final campaign in which the British Army, as the leading unit in a combination of armies brilliantly led by a French Generalissimo whom all trusted, brought down the military power of Germany. There were some six weeks of fighting after the capture of the Hindenburg line; but it was that capture—"the essential part" of the whole campaign, to use Marshal Haig's words—to which everything else was subordinate, which, in truth, decided the struggle. And the tanks are the symbol at once of the general strategy and the new tactics, by which Marshal Foch and Sir Douglas Haig, working together as only great men can, brought about this result, bettered all that they had learned from Germany, and proved themselves the master minds of the war. For the tanks mean *surprise—mobility—*the power to break off any action when it has done its part, and rapidly to transfer the attack somewhere else. Behind them, indeed, stood all the immense resources of the British artillery—guns of all calibres, so numerous that in many a great attack they stood wheel to wheel in a continuous arc of fire. But it was the tanks which cleared the way, which flattened the wire, and beat down the skill and courage of the German machine gunners, who have taken such deadly toll of British life during the war. And behind the tanks, protected also by that creeping barrage of the great guns, which was the actual invention of that famous Army Commander with whom I had spent an evening at Valenciennes, came the infantry lines, those now seasoned and victorious troops, for whose "stubborn greatness in defence," no less than their "persistent vigour" and "relentless determination" in attack, General Haig finds words that every now and then, though very rarely, betray the emotion of the great leader who knows that he has been well and loyally served. There is even a certain jealousy of the tanks, I notice, among the men who form the High Command of the Army, lest they should in any way detract from the credit of the men. "Oh, the tanks—yes—very useful, of course—but the *men!*—it was the quality of the infantry did it."

All the same, the tanks—or rather these tell-tale marks beside this front trench of the Hindenburg line, together with that labyrinth of trenches, cut by the Canal du Nord, which fills the whole eastern scene to the horizon—remain in my mind as somehow representative of the two main facts which, according to all one can read and all one can gather from the living voices of those who know, dominated the last stage of the war.

For what are those facts?

First, the combination in battle after battle, on the British front, of the strategical genius, at once subtle and simple, of Marshal Foch, with the supreme tactical skill of the British

Commander-in-Chief.

Secondly, the decisive importance to the ultimate issue, of this great fortified zone of country lying before my eyes in the winter twilight; which stretches, as my map tells me, right across Northern France, from the Ypres salient, in front of Lille and Douai, through this point south-west of Cambrai where I am standing, and again over those distant slopes to the south-west over which the shades are gathering, to St. Quentin and St. Gobain. These miles of half-effaced and abandoned trenches, with all those scores of other miles to the north-west and the south-east which the horizon covers, represent, as I have said, the culminating effort of the war; the last effective stand of the German brought to bay; the last moment when Ares, according to Greek imagination, "the money changer of war," who weighs in his vast balance the lives of men, still held the balance of this mighty struggle in some degree uncertain. But the fortress fell; the balance came down on the side of the Allies, and from that moment, though there was much fighting still to do, the war was won.

As to the actual meaning in detail of the "Hindenburg" or "Siegfried" line, let me, for the benefit of those who have never seen even a yard of it, come back to the subject presently, helped by a captured German document, and by a particularly graphic description of it, written by an officer of the First Army.

But first, with the scene still before me—the broken bridge, the ruined lock, the splendid trench at my feet, and those innumerable white lines on the far hill-side—let me recall the great story of the six months which preeceded the attack of Sir Julian Byng's Third Army on this bank of the Canal du Nord.

It was on Monday, March 25th, that at Doullens, a small manufacturing town, lying in a wooded and stream-fed hollow not far from Amiens, there took place the historic meeting of the leading politicians and generals of the war, which ended in the appointment of Marshal Foch to the supreme military command of the Allied forces in France. I remember passing Doullens in 1917, dipping down into the hollow, climbing out of it again on to the wide upland leading to Amiens, and idly noticing the picturesqueness of the place. But there must be a house and a room in Doullens, which ought already to be marked as national property, and will certainly be an object of travel in years to come for both English and French; no less than that factory to the west of Verdun where Castelnau and Petain conferred at the sharpest crisis of the immortal siege. For there—so it is generally believed—the practical sense and generous temper of the British Commander brought about that change in the whole condition of the war which we know as the "unity of command." Sunday, March 24th, had been a particularly bad day in that vast defensive battle which, in General Haig's phrase, "strained the resources of the Allies to the uttermost." There had been difficulties and misunderstandings also—perfectly natural in the circumstances—with the French Army on the right of the British line. Yet never was a perfect co-ordination of the whole Allied effort in face of the German attack so absolutely essential.

Sir Douglas Haig took the lead. A year before this date he had refused in other circumstances, as one supremely responsible for the British Army, to agree to a unified command under a French general, and the events had justified him. But now the hour had arrived, and the man. The proposal that General Foch should take the supreme control of the four Allied armies now fighting or gathering in France was made and pressed by Sir Douglas Haig. There was anxious debate, some opposition in unexpected quarters, and finally a unanimous decision. General Foch, waiting in an adjoining room, was called in and accepted the task with the simplicity of the great soldier who is also a man of religious faith. For Foch, the devout Catholic and pupil of the Jesuits, and Haig the Presbyterian, are alike in this: there rules in both of them the conviction that this world is not an aimless scene of chance, and that man has an Unseen Helper.

Such, at least, is the story as it runs; and, at any rate, from that meeting at Doullens dates the transformation of the war. For five weeks afterwards the German attack beat against the British front, bending and denting but never breaking it. Then at the end of April the attack died down, brought up against the British and French reserves which Ludendorff had immensely underrated, and—strategically—it had failed.

A month later came the "violent surprise attack" on the Aisne, which, as we all know, carried the enemy to the Marne and across it, and on the 7th of June the French were again attacked between Noyon and Montdidier. The strain was great. But Foch was making his plans; the British Army was being steadily reorganised; the drafts from England were being absorbed and trained under a Commander-in-Chief who, by the consent of all his subordinates, is a supreme manipulator and trainer of fighting men, while never forgetting the human reality which is the foundation of it all. Soon the number of effective infantry divisions on the British front had risen from forty-five to fifty-two. And meanwhile American energy was pouring men across the Atlantic, and everywhere along the Allied front and in the Allied countries, but especially in ravaged, war-weary France, the news of the weekly arrivals, 80,000, 100,000, 70,000 men, was exactly the stimulus that the older armies needed.

It was a race between the German Army and the growing strength of the Allies—and it was presently a duel between Ludendorff and Foch. "Attack! attack!" was the German military cry, "or it will be too late!" And on July 15th Ludendorff struck again to the east and south-west of Rheims. General Gouraud, who was in command of the Fourth French Army to the east of Rheims, told me at Strasbourg the dramatic story of that attack and of its brilliant and over-whelming repulse. I will return to it in a later letter. Meanwhile the German Command in the Marne salient plunged blindly on, deepening the pocket in which his forces were engaged—striking for Montmirail, Meaux, and Paris.

But Foch's hour had come, and on July 18th he launched that

ever-famous counter-offensive on the Soissons-Chateau-Thierry front, which, in Sir Douglas Haig's quiet words, "effected a complete change in the whole military situation."

After a moment of bewilderment, attacked on both flanks by irresistible forces of French, British, and Americans, von Boehm turned to escape from the hounds on his track. He fought, as we all know, a skilful retreat to the Vesle, leaving prisoners and guns all the way, and on the Vesle he stood. But the last German offensive was done, and Foch was already thinking of other prey.

On the 23rd of July there was another conference of the military leaders, held under other omens, and in a different atmosphere from that of March 25th. At that conference Foch disclosed his plans and gave each army its task. The French and American Armies—the American Army now in all men's mouths because of its gallant and distinguished share in the June and July fighting on the Marne—were to attack towards Mezieres and Metz, while the British Armies struck towards St. Quentin and Cambrai—in other words, looked onward to the final grapple with the "great fortified zone known as the Hindenburg line." So long as Germany held that she was undefeated. With that gone she was at the mercy of the Allies.

But much had to be done before the Hindenburg line could be attacked. Foch and Haig, with Debeney, Mangin, Gouraud, and Pershing in support, played a great *arpeggio*—it is Mr. Buchan's word, and a most graphic one—on the linked line of the Allies. On the British front four great battles, involving the capture of more than 100,000 prisoners and hundreds of guns, had to be fought before the Hindenburg line was reached. They followed each other in quick succession, brilliantly intercalated or supported by advances on the French and American fronts, Mangin on the Aisne, Gouraud in Champagne, Pershing at St. Mihiel.

The Battle of Amiens (August 8th-13th), fought by the Fourth British Army under General Rawlinson, and the First French

Army under General Debeney, who had been placed by Marshal Foch under the British command, carried the line of the Allies twelve miles forward in a vital sector, liberated Amiens and the Paris-Amiens railway, and resulted in the capture of 22,000 prisoners and 400 guns, together with the hurried retreat of the enemy from wide districts to the south, where the French were on his heels. These were great days for the Canadian and Australian troops. Four Canadian divisions under Sir Arthur Currie, on the right of an eleven-mile front, four Australian divisions under Sir John Monash in the centre, with the Third British Corps under General Butler on the left, led the splendid advance. The Field Marshal in his dispatch speaks of the "brilliant and predominating part" played by the two Dominion Corps—the "skill and determination of the infantry," the "fine performance" of the cavalry. By this victory the British Army recovered the initiative it had temporarily lost. All was changed. And even more striking than the actual gains in ground, prisoners, and guns, was the effect upon the *morale* of both German and British troops. The Germans could hardly believe their defeat; the British exultantly knew that their hour had come.

In *the Battle of Bapaume* (August 21st-September 1st) the Third and Fourth British Armies, twenty-three divisions against thirty-five German divisions, drove the enemy from one side of the old Somme battle-field to the other, recovered all the ground lost in the spring, and took 34,000 prisoners and 270 guns. The enemy's *morale* was now failing; surrenders became frequent, and there were many signs of the exhaustion of the German reserves. And again, by the turning of his line, large tracts of territory were recovered almost without fighting. By September 6th, five months after we had stood "with our backs to the wall" in defence of the Channel ports, the Lys salient had disappeared, and the old Ypres line was almost restored.

In *the Battle of the Scarpe* (August 26th-September 3rd) General Horne's First Army, with the Canadian Corps and the Highlanders in its ranks, drove eastwards, north and south of

Mrs. Humphry Ward

the Scarpe, till they had come within striking distance of the Drocourt-Queant line. In twelve hours, on the 2nd of September, the Canadian Corps, with forty tanks, Canadian cavalry and armoured cars, had captured "the whole of the elaborate system of wire, trenches, and strong points," which runs north-west from the Hindenburg line proper to the Lens defences at Drocourt; while the 17th Corps attacked the triangle of fortifications marking the junction of the Drocourt-Queant line with the Hindenburg line proper, and cleared it magnificently, the 52nd (Lowland) Division especially distinguishing itself. There was "stern fighting" further south that day, right down to the neighbourhood of Peronne; but during the night the enemy "struck his tents," and began a hasty retreat to the line of the Canal du Nord. Sixteen thousand prisoners and 200 guns had been the spoil of the battle.

The Battle of Havrincourt (September 12th-18th) was a struggle for the outer defences of the Hindenburg line, which had to be carried before the line itself could be dealt with. Six days secured the positions wanted for the final attack, and in those six days fifteen British divisions had defeated twenty German divisions, and captured nearly 12,000 prisoners and 100 guns.

That rapid summary has brought me back to the point from which I started. In three months and a half the "mighty conflict," in which, on the British side, something short of 700,000 bayonets were engaged, had rushed on from victory to victory; Foch and Haig working together in an ideal marriage of minds and resources; the attack retaining everywhere by the help of the tanks—of which, in the Battle of Amiens, General Rawlinson had 400 under his command—the elements of surprise and mobility. The harassed enemy would find himself hard pressed in a particular section, driven to retreat, with heavy losses in ground, guns and prisoners; and then, as soon as he had discovered a line on which to stand and had thrown in his reserves, the attack would be broken off, only to begin again elsewhere, and with the same energy, unexpectedness, and success. British Staff work and British tactics were at their highest point of excellence, and the spirit of the men, fanned by that breeze which Victory and Hope bring with them, were, in the Commander-in-Chief's word, "magnificent."

And so we come to the evening of the 26th of September. Along these hill-sides, where we stand, on the west side of the Canal du Nord, lay Sir Julian Byng and the Third Army. To his right, on the south-east, was General Rawlinson, facing the strongest portion of the Hindenburg line, with two American divisions, led by Major-General Read, under his command; while on his left, and to the north, the First Army, under General Home, held the line along the Canal du Nord, and the marshes of the Sensee.

The most critical moment in the campaign had arrived. For in the assault on the Hindenburg line heavy risks had to be run. It is clear, I think, from the wording of Marshal Haig's dispatch, that in respect to the attack he took a special responsibility, which was abundantly vindicated by the event. The British War Cabinet was extremely anxious; the French Generalissimo was content to leave it to the British Commander-in-Chief; and Sir Douglas Haig, confident "that the British attack was the essential part of the general scheme, and that the moment was favourable," had the decision to make, and made it as we know. It is evident also from the dispatch that Sir Douglas was quite aware, not only of the military, but of the political risk. "The political effects of an unsuccessful attack upon a position so well known as the Hindenburg line would be large, and would go far to revive the declining *morale*, not only of the German Army, but of the German people." This aspect of the matter must, of course, have been terribly present to the mind of the British War Cabinet.

Moreover, the British Armies had been fighting continuously for nearly two months, and their losses, though small in proportion to what had been gained and to the prisoners taken, were still considerable.

Nevertheless, with all these considerations in mind, "*I decided*," says General Haig, "*to proceed with the attack*."[6]

[6] The italics are mine.

There lie before me a Memorandum, by an officer of the General Staff, on the Hindenburg line, drawn up about a month after the capture of the main section of it, and also a German report, made by a German officer in the spring of 1917. The great fortified system, as it subsequently became, was then incomplete. It was begun late in 1916, when, after the battle of the Somme, the German High Command had determined on the retreat which was carried out in February and March of the following year. It was dug by Russian prisoners, and the forced labour of French and Belgian peasants. The best engineering and tactical brains of the German Army went to its planning; and both officers and men believed it to be impregnable. The whole vast system was from four miles to seven miles deep, one interlocked and inter-communicating system of trenches, gun emplacements, machine-gun positions, fortified villages, and the rest, running from north-west to south-east across France, behind the German lines. In front of the British forces, writes an officer of the First Army, before the capture of the Drocourt-Queant portion of the line, ran "line upon line, mile upon mile, of defences such as had never before been imagined; system after complicated system of trenches, protected with machine-gun positions, with trench mortars, manned by a highly-trained infantry, and by machine-gunners unsurpassed for skill and courage. The whole was supported by artillery of all calibres. The defences were the result of long-trained thought and of huge work. They had been there unbroken for years; and they had been constantly improved and further organised." And the great canals—the Canal du Nord and the Scheldt Canal, but especially the latter, were worked into the system with great skill, and strongly fortified. It is evident indeed that the mere existence of this fortified line gave a certain high confidence to the German Army, and that when it was captured, that confidence, already severely shaken, finally crumbled and broke. Indeed, by the time the British Armies had captured the covering portions of the line, and stood in front of the line itself, the *morale* of the German Army as a whole was no longer equal to holding it. For our casualties in taking it, though severe, were far less than we had suffered in the battle of the Scarpe; and one detects in some of our reports, when the victory was won, a certain amazement that we had been let off—comparatively—so lightly. Nevertheless, if there had been any failure in attack, or preparation, or leadership, we should have paid dearly for it; and a rally on the Hindenburg line, had we allowed the enemy any chance of it, might have prolonged the war for months. But there was no failure, and there was no rally. Never had our tried Army leaders, General Horne, General Byng, and General Rawlinson carried out more brilliantly the general scheme of the two supreme Commanders; never was the Staff work better; never were the subordinate services more faultlessly efficient. An American officer who had served with distinction in the British Army before the entry of his own country into the war, spoke to me in Paris with enthusiasm of the British Staff work during this three months' advance. "It was simply *marvellous!*—People don't understand." "Everything was ready," writes an eyewitness of the First Army.[7] The rapidity of our advance completely surprised the enemy, some of whose batteries were captured as they were coming into action. Pontoon and trestle bridges were laid across the canal with lightning speed. The engineers, coming close behind the firing line, brought up the railways, light and heavy, as though by magic—built bridges, repaired roads. The Intelligence Staff, in the midst of all this rapid movement "gathered and forwarded information of the enemy's forces in front, his divisions, his reserves, his intentions." Telephones and telegraphs were following fast on the advance, connecting every department, whether stationary or still on the move. News was coming in at every moment— of advances, captures, possibilities in new country, casualties, needs. All these were being considered and collated by the Staff, decisions taken and orders sent out.

[7] The following paragraphs are based on the deeply

Mrs. Humphry Ward

interesting account of the First Army operations of last year, written by Captain W. Inge, Intelligence and Publicity Officer on Sir Henry Home's Staff.

Meanwhile divisions were being relieved, billets arranged for, transport organised along the few practicable roads. Ambulances were coming and going. Petrol must be accessible everywhere; breakdown gangs and repair lorries must be ready always to clear roads, and mend bridges. And the men doing these jobs must be handled, fed, and directed, as well as the fighting line.

Letters came and went. The men were paid. Records of every kind were kept. New maps were made, printed, and sent round—and quickly, since food and supplies depended on them. "One breakdown on a narrow road, one failure of an important message over a telephone wire—and how much may depend on it!"

"Yet thanks to intelligent and devoted work, to experience and resource, how little in these later stages of the war has gone wrong!"

The fighting men, the Staff work, the auxiliary services of the British Army—the long welding of war had indeed brought them by last autumn to a wonderful efficiency. And that efficiency was never so sharply tested as by the exchange of a stationary war for a war of movement. The Army swept on "over new but largely devastated country," into unknown land, where all the problems, as compared with the long years of trench war, were new. Yet nothing failed—"except the astounded enemy's power of resistance."

So much from a first-hand record of the First Army's advance. It carries me back as I summarise it to my too brief stay at Valenciennes, and the conversations of the evening with the Army Commander and several members of his Staff. The talk turned largely on this point of training, Staff work, and general efficiency. There was no boasting whatever; but one read the pride of gallant and devoted men in the forces they had commanded. "Then we have not muddled through?" I said, laughing, to the Army Commander. Sir Henry smiled. "No, indeed, we have *not* muddled through!"

And the results of this efficiency were soon seen. Take first the attack of the First and Third Armies on this section. North of Moeuvres the Canadians, under General Home, crossing the Canal in the early morning of September 27th, on a narrow front, and spreading out behind the German troops holding the Canal, by a fan-shaped manoeuvre, brilliantly executed, which won reluctant praise from captured German officers, pushed on for Bourlon and Cambrai. The 11th Division, following close behind, turned northward, with our barrage from the heavy guns, far to the west, protecting their left flank, towards the enemy line along the Sensee, taking ground and villages as they went. Meanwhile the front German line, pinned between our barrage behind them and the Canal, taken in front and rear, and attacked by the 56th Division, had nothing to do but surrender.

"The day's results," says my informant of the First Army, "were the great Hindenburg system (in this northern section) finally broken, the height before Cambrai captured, thousands of prisoners and great quantities of guns taken, and our line at its furthest point 7,000 yards nearer Germany. A great triumph!"

Meanwhile in the centre—just where I have asked the reader of this paper to stand with me in imagination on the hill-side overlooking the Canal du Nord—General Byng's Third Army, including the Guards' Division, forced the Canal crossings in face of heavy fire, and moving forward towards Cambrai in the half light of dawn, took trenches and villages from the fighting and retreating enemy. After the forward troops were over, the engineers rushed on, bridging the Canal, under the fire of the German guns, rapidly clearing a way for infantry and supplies. A map issued by the Tank Corps shows that close to this point on the Cambrai-Bapaume road six tanks were operating—

among them no doubt that agile fellow, whose tracks still show on the hillside!—while on the whole front of the Third and First Armies sixty-five tanks were in action. By the end of that long day 10,000 prisoners had been taken, and 200 guns, an earnest of what was to follow.

It was on the front of the Fourth Army, however, in the section from St. Quentin to Gouzeaucourt, that the heaviest blow was planned by the Commander-in-Chief. Here the "exceptional strength of the enemy's position made a prolonged bombardment necessary." So while the First and Third Armies were advancing, on the north, with a view to lightening the task of the Fourth Army, for forty-eight hours General Rawlinson maintained a terrible bombardment, which drove the defenders of the famous line underground, and cut them off from food and supplies. And on the morning of the 29th the Fourth Army attacked.

But I have no intention of repeating in any detail the story of that memorable day. The exploit of the 46th Division under General Boyd, in swimming and capturing the southern section of the Canal below Bellenglise, will long rank as one of the most amazing stories of the war. Down the steep banks clambered the men, flung themselves into the water, and with life-belts, and any other aid that came handy, crossed the Canal under fire, and clambered up the opposite bank. And the achievement is all the more welcome to British pride in British pluck, when it is remembered that, according to the German document I have already quoted, it was an impossible one. "The deep canal cutting from the southern end of the canal tunnel ... with its high steep banks constitutes a strong obstacle. *The enemy will hardly attack here.*" So writes the German officer describing the line.

But it was precisely here that "the enemy" did attack!— capturing prisoners (4,000 of them by the end of the day, with 70 guns) and German batteries in action, before the German Command had had time to realise the direction of the attack.It was not, however, at this point that the severest fighting of the battle occurred. Across the great tunnel to the north of Bellicourt, where the Canal passes for nearly two miles underground, ran the main Hindenburg system, carrying it eastwards over the Canal itself, and it was here that the fiercest resistance was put up. The two American divisions had the post of honour and led the advance. It was a heavy task, largely owing to the fact that it had not been possible to master the German outpost line completely before the advance started, and numerous small bodies of the enemy, left behind in machine-gun posts, tunnels, and dug-outs, were able to harass it seriously for a time. But the "Americans fought like lions" —how often I heard that phrase from our own men in France! The American losses were no doubt higher than would have been the case with more experienced troops, seasoned by long fighting,—so I have understood from officers present at the battle. It was perhaps partly because of "their eagerness to push on" without sufficiently clearing up the ground behind them that they lost so heavily, and that advanced elements of the two divisions were for a time cut off. But nothing daunted these fresh and gallant men. Their sacrifices, as Marshal Haig has recently said, addressing General O'Ryan, who comman-ded the 27th Division in this fight, were "made with a courage and devotion unsurpassed in all the dread story of this war. The memory of our great attack on the Hindenburg line on September 29th, 1918, in which the 27th American division, with troops from all parts of the British Empire, took so gallant and glorious a part, will never die, and the service then rendered by American troops will be remembered with gratitude and admiration throughout the British Empire."

That misty September day marks indeed a culminating moment in the history of the Empire and the war. It took six more days of sharp fighting to capture the last remnants of the Hindenburg line, and six more weeks before Germany, beaten and demoralised by sea and land, accepted the Armistice terms imposed by the Allies. But on September 29th, the war was for all practical purposes won. General Gouraud at the time was making his brilliant advance in Champagne. The Americans were pushing forward in the Argonne. Both movements were indispensable; but it was the capture of this great fortified system which really decided the war. "No attack in the history of the world, was ever better carried out," said Marshal Foch to Mr. Ward Price, in Paris, on April 16th last—"than the one made on the Hindenburg line near St. Quentin and Cambrai, by the Fourth, Third and First British Armies, on September 27th-29th. The enemy positions were most formidable. Nothing could stop the British. They swept right over them. It was a glorious day for British arms." It was also the climax of two months' fighting in which French, British, and Americans had all played to the full the part laid down for them by the history of the preceding years, and in which it fell to the British Army to give the final and victorious blow.

Non nobis, Domine!—non nobis!

It will, I think, be of use to the non-military reader if I append to the sketch I have just given of the last phase of the British effort, the following paragraphs written last January by an officer of the General Staff, in response to the question indicated in the opening sentence.

"I have been asked to say what in my opinion were the most critical and anxious stages of the series of great successful battles opened on the 8th August, 1918. The question is not easy, for the whole period was one of high tension, calling for continuous and unsparing effort.

"From one point of view, the opening battle east of Amiens was decisive, for it marked the turning point of the campaign on the British front. Its moral effects, both on our own troops and on the enemy, were far-reaching and give the key to the whole of the succeeding struggle. Nothing less than a sweeping success, such as that actually achieved, could have produced this result. The days preceding the attack, therefore, constituted a most anxious period. On the other hand, from the purely military point of view, our chances of success were exceedingly good. The attack was to be delivered by fresh troops, second to none in the world in fighting qualities, assisted by an unprecedented concentration of mechanical aids to victory. Preparations had been long and careful, every contingency had been thought out, and there was every reason to expect that our attack would be a complete surprise.

"Militarily, the more critical period was that which immediately followed the battle when, having reached the line of the old Somme defences of 1916, it was decided to switch the point of attack to the area north of the Somme. On the success of this manoeuvre depended whether the attack of the 8th August was to be a single isolated victory comparable to the battle of Messines in June, 1917, or whether it was to develop into something very much greater. The decision was a grave one, and was in some sense a departure from previous practice. The enemy was now on the alert, the troops to be employed had already been severely tried in the earlier fighting of the year, and failure would have called down severe criticism upon the wisdom of abandoning so quickly the scene of our first great success.

"It was only after the first days of heavy fighting (in the battle of Bapaume), during which progress was comparatively slow and the situation full of anxiety, that the event proved that the step had been wisely taken.

"Then, when the success of this bold manoeuvre had declared itself, and the enemy had begun the first stages of his great retreat, the next critical period arrived on the 2nd September, when the powerful defences of the Drocourt-Queant line were attacked and broken. The effect of this success was to render the whole of the enemy's positions to the south untenable and to throw him back definitely upon the Hindenburg line.

"Undoubtedly the most critical and anxious period of the whole advance arrived at the end of September. The culminating attacks of the 27th and 29th of that month on the Canal du Nord and Hindenburg line defences shattered the most formidable series of field defences that military science has yet devised and drove the enemy into open country. These attacks, indeed, accomplished far more than this. They definitely broke the power of resistance of the German Armies in the field. In the battles which followed, our troops were able to take greater and greater risks, and on every occasion with complete success.

"Yet again, the risk was great. If the enemy had succeeded in holding the Hindenburg position, he would have been little, if anything, worse off, territorially at any rate, than he had been before he began his great adventure of the spring. It was clearly a time for him to pull himself together and hold on at all costs.

"On the other hand and with all its difficulties, so favourable an opportunity of securing immediate and decisive victory, by pressing our advantage, could scarcely be expected to present itself again. The decision was therefore taken and was justified by success.

"After this battle, our chief anxieties lay rather in the ability of our supply system to keep pace with our Armies than in any resistance that the enemy could offer. In the succeeding battles our troops accomplished with comparative ease feats which earlier in the struggle it would have been madness to attempt; and in the final battle of the war, begun on the 4th November, the crossing of the Sambre and the clearing of the great Mormal Forest furnished a wonderful tribute to the complete ascendency which their earlier victories had enabled our troops to establish over the enemy."

CHAPTER IV

GENERAL GOURAUD AT STRASBOURG

The Maine—Verdun—Champagne—it is in connection with these three names that the French war consciousness shows itself most sensitive and most profound, just as the war consciousness of Great Britain vibrates most deeply when you test it with those other names—Ypres—Arras—the Somme—Cambrai. As is the name of Ypres to the Englishman, so is that of Verdun to the Frenchman, invested even with a more poignant significance, since the countryside where so many sons of France laid down their lives was their own adored mother-land, indivisibly part of themselves, as those grim, water-logged flats north and south of the Menin road could never be to a Lancashire or London boy. And no other French battle-field wears for a Frenchman quite the same aureole that shines for ever on those dark, riven hills of Verdun. But it seemed to me that in the feeling of France, Champagne came next—Champagne, associated first of all with Castelnau's victory in the autumn of 1915, then with General Nivelle's tragic check in 1917, with the serious crisis in the French Army in May and June of that year; and finally with General Gouraud's brilliant successes in the summer and autumn of 1918.

Six weeks ago I found myself in Strasbourg, where General Gouraud is in command of the Fourth Army, now stationed in Alsace. Through a long and beautiful day we had driven south from Metz, across the great fortified zone to the south of that town; with its endless trenches and wire-fields, its camouflaged roads, its railway stations packed with guns, its ammunition dumps and battery-emplacements, which Germany had prepared at the outset of the war, and which still awaited the Americans last November, had the Allies' campaign not ended when it did. There was a bright sun on all the wide and lovely landscape, on the shining rivers, the flooded spaces and the old towns, and magnificent clouds lay piled above the purple Vosges, to the south and east. We caught up a French division on the march, with long lines of lorries, artillery wagons, guns and field-kitchens, and as our car got tangled up with it in passing through the small towns and villages, we had ample time to notice the behaviour of the country-folk, and the reception given to the troops. Nothing, it seemed to me, could have been warmer and more spontaneous, especially as soon as we crossed the boundary of Alsace. The women came running out to their door-steps, the children formed a tumultuous escort, men and women peered smiling out of the covered country carts, and tradesmen left their counters to see the show.

At Metz I was conscious of a hostile and bitter element in the town, not to be wondered at when one remembers that Metz has a population of 25,000 immigrant Germans out of a population of less than 70,000. But in the country towns of Alsace and in Strasbourg itself, my own impression, for what it is worth, was everywhere an impression of solid and natural rejoicing in the new order of things. That there are a large number of Germans in Strasbourg and Alsace generally is, of course, true. There were some 450,000 before the war, out of a population of rather more than two millions, and there are now at a rough estimate about 300,000, of whom nearly 100,000 are to be found in Metz and Strasbourg. The whole administration of the two provinces, with very few exceptions, was a German administration, imported from Germany, and up to the outbreak of war, the universities and the schools— *i.e.*, the whole teaching profession—were German, and many of the higher clergy. The leading finance of the provinces was German. And so on. But I cannot see any reason to doubt that the real feeling of the native population in the two provinces, whether in town or country, has remained throughout these forty-eight years strongly and passionately French. "Since when did you expect the French to come back?" asked M. Mirman, the present Commissioner of the French Republic at Metz, of an old peasant whom he came across not long ago on an official inspection. The old man's eyes kindled—"*Depuis toujours!*" he said—"I knew it would come, but I was afraid it mightn't come till I was dead, so I used to say to my son: 'If I am dead, and the French come back, you will go to the cemetery, you will knock three times on my grave—I shall hear!' And my son promised."

My present concern, however, is not with the Alsace-Lorraine question, but with the brilliant Army Commander who now occupies what used to be the Headquarters of the German Army Corps which held Alsace. My acquaintance with him was due to a piece of audacity on my part. The record of General Gouraud in Champagne, and at the Dardanelles, was well known to me, and I had heard much of his attractive and romantic personality. So, on arriving at our hotel after a long day's motoring, and after consulting with the kind French Lieutenant who was our escort, I ventured a little note to the famous General. I said I had been the guest of the British Army for six days on our front, and was now the guest of the French Army, for a week, and to pass through Strasbourg without seeing the victor of the "front de Champagne" would be tantalising indeed. Would he spare an Englishwoman, whose love for the French nation had grown with her growth and strengthened with her years, twenty minutes of his time?

The note was sent and I waited, looking out the while on the gay and animated crowd that filled the Platz Gutenberg in front of the hotel, and listening to the bands of children, shouting the "Marseillaise," and following every French officer as he appeared. Was there ever a more lovely winter evening? A rosy sunset seemed to have descended into the very streets and squares of the beautiful old town. Wisps of pink cloud were tangled in the narrow streets, against a background of intensely blue sky. The high-roofed burgher houses, with their decorated fronts, had an "unsubstantial faery" look, under the strange rich light; and the front of the Cathedral, with its single delicate spire, soared, one suffusion of rose, to an incredible height above the narrow street below.

"*Allons, enfants de la patri-e!*" But a motor-car is scattering the children, and an *ordonnance* descends. A note, written by the General's own left hand—he lost his right arm in consequence of a wound at the Dardanelles—invites us to dinner with him and his staff forthwith—the motor will return for us. So, joyously, we made what simple change we could, and in another hour or so we were waiting in the General's study for the great man to appear. He came at once, and I look back upon the evening that followed as one of the most interesting that Fate has yet sent my way.

As he entered I saw a man of slight, erect figure, lame, indeed, and with that sad, empty sleeve, but conveying an immediate and startling impression as of some fiery, embodied force, dominating the slender frame. He had a short beard, brown and silky, dark hair, and a pair of clear blue eyes, shrewd, indeed, and penetrating, but singularly winning. A soldier, a most modern soldier, yet with an infusion of something romantic, a touch of thoughtful or melancholy charm that recalled old France. He was dressed in a dark blue mess coat, red breeches, and top boots, with three or four orders sparkling on his breast. His manners were those of an old-fashioned and charming courtesy.

As is well known, like Marshal Foch and General Castelnau, General Gouraud is a Catholic. And like General Mangin, the great Joffre himself, Gallieni, Franchet d'Esperey, d'Humbert, and other distinguished leaders of the French Army, he made his reputation in the French Colonial service. In Morocco, and the neighbouring lands, where he spent some twenty-two years, from 1892 to 1914, he was the right-hand of General Lyautey, and conspicuous no less for his humanity, his peace-making, and administrative genius than for his brilliant services in the field. When the war broke out General Lyautey indeed tried for a time to keep him at his side. But the impulse of the younger soldier was too strong; and his chief at last let him go. Gouraud arrived in France just after the Marne victory, and was at once given the command of a division in the Argonne. He spent the first winter of the war in that minute study of the ground, and that friendly and inspiring intercourse with his soldiers, which have been two of the marked traits of his career, and when early in 1915 he was transferred to Champagne, as Commander of a Corps d'Armee, he had time, before he was called away, to make a survey of the battle-field east of Rheims, which was of great value to him later when he came to command the Fourth French Army in the same district. But meanwhile came the summons to the Dardanelles, where, as we all remember, he served with the utmost loyalty and good will under General Sir Ian Hamilton. He replaced General d'Amade on the 10th of May, led a brilliant and successful attack on the 4th of June, and was, alas! terribly wounded before the end of the month. He was entering a dressing-station close to his headquarters to which some wounded French soldiers had just been brought when a shell exploded beside him. His aide-de-camp was knocked over, and when he picked himself up, stunned and bewildered, he saw his General lying a few yards away, with both legs and an arm broken. Gouraud, during these few weeks, had already made his mark, and universal sympathy from French and English followed him home. His right arm was amputated on the way to Toulon; the left leg, though broken below the knee, was not seriously injured, but the fracture of the right involved injury to the hip, and led to permanent lameness.

Who would have imagined that a man so badly hurt could yet have afterwards become one of the most brilliant and successful generals in the French Army? The story of his recovery must rank with the most amazing instances of the power of the human will, and there are various touches connected with it in current talk which show the temper of the man, and the love which has been always felt for him. One of his old masters of the College Stanislas who went to meet him at the station on his arrival at Paris, and had been till then unaware of the extent of the General's wounds, could not conceal his emotion at seeing him. "*Eh, c'est le sort des batailles,*" said Gouraud gaily, to his pale and stumbling friend. "One would have said he was two men in one," said another old comrade—"one was betrayed to me by his works; the other spoke to me in his words." The legends of him in hospital are many. He was determined to walk again—and quickly. "One has to teach these legs," he said impatiently, "to walk naturally, not like machines." Hence the steeple-chases over all kinds of obstacles—stools, cushions, chairs—that his nurses must needs arrange for him in the hospital passages; and later on his determined climbing of any hill that presented itself—at first leaning on his mother (General Gouraud has never married), then independently.

He was wounded at the end of June, 1915. At the beginning of November he was sent at the head of a French Military Mission to Italy, and on his return in December was given the command of the Fourth French Army, the Army of Champagne. There on that famous sector of the French line, where Castelnau and Langle de Cary in the autumn of the same year had all but broken through, he remained through the whole of 1916. That was the year of Verdun and the Somme. Neither the Allies nor the enemy had men or energy to spare for important action in Champagne that year; but Gouraud's watch was never surprised, and again he was able to acquaint himself with every military feature, and every local peculiarity of the desolate chalk-hills where France has buried so many thousands of her sons. At the end of 1916, his old chief, General Lyautey, now French Minister for War, insisted on his going back to Morocco as Governor; but happily for the Army of Champagne, the interlude was short, and by the month of May, Lyautey was once more in Morocco and Gouraud in Champagne—to remain there in command of his beloved Fourth Army till the end of the war.

* * * * *

Such then, in brief outline, was the story of the great man whose guests we were proud to be on that January evening. Dinner was very animated and gay. The rooms of the huge building was singularly bare, having been stripped by the Germans before their departure of everything portable. But *en revanche* the entering French, finding nothing left in the fine old house, even of the *mobilier* which had been left there in 1871, discovered a *chateau* belonging to the Kaiser close by, and requisitioned from it some of the necessaries of life. Bordeaux drunk out of a glass marked with the Kaiser's monogram had a taste of its own. In the same way, when on the British front we drew up one afternoon, north of St. Omer, at a level crossing to let a goods train go by, I watched the interminable string of German trucks, labelled Magdeburg, Essen, Duesseldorf, and saw in them, with a bitter satisfaction, the first visible signs of the Reparation and Restitution to be.

The relations between the General and his Staff were very pleasant to watch; and after dinner there was some interesting talk of the war. I asked the General what had seemed to him the most critical moment of the struggle. He and his Chief of the Staff looked at each other gravely an instant and then the General said: "I have no doubt about it at all. Not May 27th (the break through on the Aisne)—not March 21st (the break through at St. Quentin)—but May and June, 1917—'*les mutineries dans l'armee*,' i.e., that bitter time of '*depression morale*,' as another French military critic calls it, affecting the glorious French Army, which followed on General Nivelle's campaign on the Aisne—March and April, 1917—with its high hopes of victory, its initial success, its appalling losses, and its ultimate check. Many causes combined, however—among them the leave-system in the French Army, and many grievances as to food, billeting, and the like: and the discontent was alarming and widespread. But," said General Gouraud, "Petain stepped in and saved the situation." "How?" one asked. "*Il s'occupa du soldat*—(he gave his mind to the soldier) —that was all." The whole leave-system was transformed, the food supply and the organisation of the Army canteens were immensely improved—pay was raised—and everything was done that could be done, while treating actual mutiny with a stern hand, to meet the soldiers' demands. "In our army," said General Gouraud, "a system of discipline like that of the German Army is impossible. We are a democracy. We must have the consent of the governed. In the last resort the soldier must be able to say: '*J'obeis d'amitie.*'"

That great result, according to General Gouraud, was finally achieved by General Petain's reforms. He gave as a proof of it that on the night of the Armistice, he and his Staff, at Chalons, unable to sit still indoors, went out and mingled with the crowd in the streets of that great military centre, apparently to the astonishment and pleasure of the multitude. "Everywhere along the line," said the General, "the soldiers were cheering Petain! '*Vive Petain! Vive Petain!*'" Petain was miles away; but it was the spontaneous recognition of him as the soldiers' champion and friend.

Gouraud did not say, what was no doubt the truth, that the army at Chalons were cheering Gouraud no less than Petain. For one can rarely talk with French officers about General Gouraud without coming across the statement: "He is beloved by his army. He has done so much for the soldiers." But not a word of his own share appeared in his conversation with me.

The talk passed on to the German attack on the French front in Champagne on July 15th, that perfectly-planned defence in which, to quote General Gouraud's own stirring words to his soldiers: "You broke the strength and the hopes of the enemy. That day Victory changed her camp. She has been faithful to us ever since." It makes one of the most picturesque stories of the war. The German offensive which broke out, as we know, along the whole of their new Marne front on July 15th, had been exactly anticipated for days before it began by General Gouraud and his Staff. The Fourth French Army, which Gouraud commanded, was lying to the north-east of Rheims, and the German attack on the Monts de Champagne, already the scene in 1916 and 1917 of so much desperate fighting, was meant to carry the German line down to the Marne that same day. Gouraud was amply informed by his intelligence staff, and his air service, of the enemy preparations, and had made all his own. The only question was as to the exact day and hour of the attack. Then by a stroke of good fortune, at eight o'clock on the very evening preceding the attack, twenty-seven prisoners were brought in—of whom some are said to have been Alsatian—and closely questioned by the Staff. "They told us," said Gouraud, "that the artillery attack would begin at ten minutes past midnight, and the infantry attack between three and four o'clock that very night. I thereupon gave the order for our bombardment to begin at 11.30 p.m. in order to catch the assembling German troops. I had 200 *batteries secretes* ready—of which the enemy had no idea—which had given beforehand no sign of their existence. Then we sat with our watches in our hands. Was it true—or not true? 12.5—12.6—12.8—12.9.—Probably it was a mare's nest. 12.10—*Crac!*—the bombardment had begun. We sprang to our telephones!" And presently, as the captured German officers began to come in, their French captors were listening to their bewildered astonishment "at the number of our batteries they had never discovered, which were on none of their maps, and only revealed themselves at the very moment of their own attack."

Meanwhile, the first French position was not intended to be held. The advance posts were told to delay and break up the enemy as much as possible, but the famous Monts were to be abandoned and the real resistance was to be offered on a position intermediate between the first and second position, and so densely held that no infiltration of the enemy was to be possible. Everything happened, for once, really "according to plan." The advance posts, whose order was "to sacrifice themselves," and each member of which knew perfectly well the duty laid upon him, held out—some of them—all day, and eventually fought their way back to the French lines. But on the prepared line of resistance the German attack was hopelessly broken, and men and reserves coming on fast from behind, ignorant of what had happened to the attacking troops, were mown down by the French artillery. "By midday," says the typed *compte-rendu* of operations, which,

signed by General Gouraud's own left hand, lies before me—
"the enemy appeared entirely blocked in all directions—and
the battle-position fixed by the General Commanding the
Army was intact."

Gouraud's army had, in fact, according to the proclamation of
its General, broken the attack of fifteen German divisions,
supported by ten others. The success, moreover, was of the
greatest strategical importance. Thus secured on his right, Foch
at once transferred troops from the Fourth Army, in support of
General Mangin's counter-attack of the 18th, to the other side
of the Marne salient, and Gouraud remained firmly on the
watch in the position he had so victoriously held, till the
moment came for his own advance in September.

I seem still to see him insisting—in spite of his lameness—on
bringing the Staff maps himself from his study, marking on
them the points where the fighting in the September advance
was most critical, and dictating to one of his Staff the itinerary
it would be best for us to take if we wished to see part, at least,
of the battle-field. "And you won't forget," he said, looking up
suddenly, "to go and see two things—the great cemetery at
Chalons, and the little 'Cimetiere du Mont Muret.'" He
described to me the latter, lying up in what was the main
fighting line, and how they had gathered there many of the
"unidentifiables"—the nameless, shattered heroes of a terrible
battle-field, so that they rest in the very ground where they
gave their lives. He might have told me,—but there was never
a word of it, and I only knew it later—that it was in that very
scene of desolation, from May, 1917, to March, 1918, that he
lived among his men, building up the spirit of troops that had
suffered much, physically and morally, caring for everything
that concerned them, restoring a shaken discipline and forging
the army which a year later was to fight with an iron steadiness
under its brilliant chief.

To fight both in defence and attack. From July 15th to
September 26th Gouraud remained passive in Champagne.
Then on September 26th, the day before the British attack at

Cambrai, he moved, with the First American Army on his right, against the strong German positions to the east of Rheims, which since the beginning of the war had barred the French way. In a battle of sixteen days, the French captured the whole of the fortified zone on this portion of the front, took 21,000 prisoners, 600 cannon and 3,500 machine guns. At the very same moment Sir Douglas Haig was driving through the Hindenburg line, and up to the west bank of the Selle, taking 48,000 prisoners and 600 guns; while the Americans were pushing through the difficult forest country of the Argonne, and along both sides of the Meuse.

The German strength was indeed weakening fast. Between July 16th and the Armistice, the British took 188,700 prisoners, the French 137,000, and the Americans 43,000.

CHAPTER V

ALSACE-LORRAINE

THE GLORY OF VERDUN

Before we left Strasbourg on our way to the "front de Champagne," armed with General Gouraud's maps and directions, an hour or two of most interesting conversation threw great light for me on that other "field of victory" —Alsace-Lorraine.

We brought an introduction to Dr. Pierre Bucher, a gentleman in whom Alsatian patriotism, both before the war and since the Armistice, has found one of its most effective and eloquent representatives. A man of a singularly winning and magnetic presence,—with dark, melancholy eyes, and the look of one in whom the flame of life has burnt in the past with a bitter intensity, fanned by winds of revolt and suffering. Before the war Dr. Bucher was a well-known and popular doctor in Strasbourg, recognised by Alsatian and German alike as a champion of the French spirit and French traditions in the lost provinces. He belonged to that *jeunesse* of the nineties, which, in the absence of any reasonable grounds for expecting a reversal of the events of 1871, came to the conclusion that autonomous liberties would be at any rate preferable to the naked repression, at the hands of Bismarck and Manteuffel, of the eighties and early nineties. The young men of his date decided that the whole government of the province could not any longer be left to the German bureaucrat, and a certain small number of them entered the German administration, which was imposed on the province after 1871 and had been boycotted thence-forward up to nearly the end of the century by all true Alsatians. But this line of action, where it was adopted, was taken entirely without prejudice to the national demand, which remained as firm as ever, supposing circumstances should ever admit of reunion with France.

Two causes in particular contributed to the irreconcilable attitude of the provinces:—first, the liberal tendencies of the population, the general sympathy, especially in Alsace, with the revolutionary and Napoleonic doctrines of Liberal France from 1789 onward; and secondly, the amazing lack of political intelligence shown by their new masters. "Even if you could ever have annexed us with success"—said Dr. Bucher long before the war, to a German publicist with whom he was on friendly terms—"you came, as it was, a hundred years too late. We had taken our stand with France at the Revolution. Her spirit and her traditions were ours. We were not affected by her passing fits of reaction, which never really interfered with us or our local life. Substantially the revolutionary and Napoleonic era laid the foundations of modern France, and on them we stand. They have little or nothing in common with an aristocratic and militarist Germany. Our sympathies, our traditions, our political tendencies are all French—you cannot alter them."

"But, finally—what do you expect or wish for?" said the German man of letters, after he and Dr. Bucher had talked through a great part of the night, and the German had listened to the Alsatian with an evident wish to understand Alsatian grievances.

Dr. Bucher's answer was prompt and apparently unexpected.

"Reunion with France," he said quietly—"no true Alsatian wishes anything else."

The German first stared and then threw himself back with a

good-natured laugh.

"Then indeed there's nothing to be done." (*Dann ist ja freilich gar nichts zu machen!*)

The tone was that of a strong man's patience with a dreamer; so confident did the Germans feel in their possession of the "Reichsland."

But whatever chance the Germany of Bismarck and William II. might have had of winning over Alsace-Lorriane—and it could never have been a good one—was ruined by the daily and tyrannous blundering of the German Government. The prohibition of the teaching of French in the primary schools, the immediate imposition of German military service on the newly-annexed territories, the constant espionage on all those known to hold strong sympathies with France, or views antagonistic to the German administration, the infamous passport regulations, and a hundred other grievances, deepened year by year the regret for France, and the dislike for Germany. After the first period of "protestation," marked by the constant election of "protesting" deputies to the Reichstag, came the period of repression—the "graveyard peace" of the late eighties and early nineties—followed by an apparent acquiescence of the native population. "Our young people in those years no longer sang the 'Marseillaise,'" said Dr. Bucher. Politically, the Alsatians despaired and—"we had to live together, *bon gre, mal gre*. But deep in our hearts lay our French sympathies. When I was a young student, hating my German teachers, the love for France beat in my pulses, like a ground wave" (*comme une vague de fond*).

Then after 1900 the Germans "changed greatly." They became every year richer and more arrogant; Germany from beyond the Rhine developed every year an increasing *appetit* for the native wealth and commerce of Alsace; and the methods of government became increasingly oppressive and militarist. By this time some 400,000 native Alsatians had in the course of years left the country, and about the same number of immigrant Germans had taken their places. The indifference or apathy of the old population began again to yield to more active feelings. The rise of a party definitely "Anti-Allemand," especially among the country people, made itself felt. And finally came, in Dr. Bucher's phrase, the period of "la haine" after the famous Saverne incident in 1912. That extraordinary display of German military insolence seemed to let loose unsuspected forces.

"All of a sudden, and from all sides, there was an explosion of fury against the Germans."

And as the Doctor spoke, his sensitive, charming face kindling into fire, I remembered our slow passage the day before, through the decorated streets of the beautiful old town of Saverne, in the wake of a French artillery division, and amid what seemed the spontaneous joy of a whole population!

Through all these years Dr. Bucher was a marked man in the eyes of the German authorities, but he was careful to give them no excuse for violence, and so great was his popularity, owing clearly to his humanity and self-devotion as a doctor, that they preferred to leave him alone. The German prefect once angrily said to him: "You are a real *poison* in this country, Herr Doctor!"—and not very long before the war a German official to whom he was applying for leave to invite M. Andre Tardieu to lecture in Strasbourg, broke out with pettish exasperation: "For twenty years you have been turning my hair grey, M. le Docteur!"—and permission was refused. At the outbreak of war, he naturally escaped from Strasbourg, and joined the French army; while during the latter part of the struggle, he was French military attache at Berne, and, as I understand, the head of a most successful secret service. He was one of the first Frenchmen to re-enter Strasbourg, and is now an invaluable *liaison* official between the restored French Government and the population.

The practical difficulty of the moment, in January last, was how to meet the Alsatian impatience to get rid of their

German masters, bag and baggage, while at the same time maintaining the ordinary services. Every night, meetings were being held in the Strasbourg squares to demand the immediate departure of the Germans. "*Qu'ils partent—qu'ils partent tous—et tout de suite!*" The French officials could only reply that if an immediate clearance were made of the whole German administration—"we can't run your trains—or carry your posts—or deliver your goods." But the German employes were being gradually and steadily repatriated—no doubt with much unavoidable hardship to individuals. Strasbourg contained then about 65,000 Germans out of 180,000. Among the remaining German officials there was often a curious lack of realisation of what had happened to Germany and to them. "The Germans are very *gauche*—their tone is still just the same!" And the Doctor described a scene he had witnessed in one of the bureaux of the prefecture only the day before. A German official was at his desk. Enter an Alsatian to make an inquiry about some point in a bankruptcy case. The German answered him with the curt rudeness which was the common official tone in old days, and finally, impatiently told the applicant to go. The Alsatian first opened his eyes in astonishment, and then—suddenly—flamed up. "*What!*—you think nothing is changed?—that you are the masters here as you used to be—that you can treat us as you used to treat us? We'll show you? We are the masters now. Get out of that chair!—Give it me!—while I talk to you. Behave civilly to me, *ou je vais vous flanquer un coup dans le dos!*" And the Alsatian went threateningly forward. But the German looked up—grew white—and said slowly—"Monsieur—you are right! I am at your service. What is your business?"

I asked about the amount of inter-marriage that had taken place during the forty years. Dr. Bucher thought it had been inconsiderable—and that the marriages, contracted generally between German subalterns and girls of the inn-keeping or small farming class, had been rarely happy. The Alsatian strain was the stronger, and the wife's relations despised the German intruder. "Not long before the war I came upon two small boys fighting in a back street." The boy that was getting the worst of it was abusing the other, and Dr. Bucher caught the words—"dirty Prussian!" (*sale Prussien!*) The boy at whom this was hurled, stopped suddenly, with a troubled face, as though he were going to cry. "No—no!—not me!—not me! *my father!*" Strange, tragic little tale!

As to the Church, a curious situation existed at that moment in Strasbourg. The Archbishop, a good man, of distinguished German birth, was respected and liked by his clergy, who were, however, French in sympathies almost to a man. The Archbishop, who had naturally excused himself from singing the victors' Te Deum in the Cathedral, felt that it would be wiser for him to go, and proposed to Rome that he should resign his see. His clergy, though personally attached to him, were anxious that there should be no complications with the French Government, and supported his wish to resign. But Rome had refused. Why? No doubt because the whole position of the Church and of Catholicism in these very Catholic provinces represents an important card in the hand of the Vatican, supposing the Papacy should desire at any time to reopen the Church and State question with Republican France. What is practically the regime of the Napoleonic Concordat still obtains in the recovered provinces. The clergy have always been paid by the State, and will be still paid, I understand, in spite of the Combes laws, by a special subvention, for the distribution of which the bishops will be responsible. And M. Clemenceau, as the French Prime Minister, has already nominated one or more bishops, as was the case throughout France itself up to 1905.

Everything indeed will be done to satisfy the recovered provinces that can be done. They are at present the spoiled children of France; and the poor devastated North looks on half enviously, inclined to think that "Paris forgets us!"—in the joy of the lost ones found. But Paris knows very well that there are difficulties ahead, and that the French love of symmetry and logic will have to make substantial concessions here and there to the local situation. There are a number of institutions, for instance, which have grown up and covered the country since 1871, which cannot be easily fitted to the ordinary *cadre* of French departmental government. The department would be too small a unit. The German insurance system, again, is far better and more comprehensive than the French, and will have, in one way or another, to be taken over.

But my own strong impression is that goodwill, and the Liberal *fond*, resting on the ideas of 1789, which, in spite of their Catholicism, has always existed in these eastern provinces (Metz, however, has been much more thoroughly Germanised than Strasbourg since the annexation), will see France through. And meanwhile the recovery of these rich and beautiful countries may well comfort her in some degree for her desolate fields and ruined towns of the North and Centre. The capital value of Alsace-Lorraine is put roughly at a thousand millions, and the Germans leave behind them considerable additions to the wealth of the province in the shape of new railway-lines and canals, fine stations, and public buildings, not to speak of the thousands of fruit-trees with which, in German fashion, they have lined the roads—a small, unintentional reparation for the murdered fruit-trees of the North.

*   *   *   *   *

A few days after our Strasbourg visit we drove, furnished with General Gouraud's notes and maps, up into the heart of the "front de Champagne." You cross the wide, sandy plains to the north of Chalons, with their scanty pine-woods, where Attila met his over-throw, and where the French Army has trained and manoeuvred for generations. And presently, beyond the great military camp of pre-war days, you begin to mount into a region of chalk hills, barren and lonely enough before the war, and now transformed by the war into a scene which almost rivals the Ypres salient and Verdun itself in tragic suggestiveness. Standing in the lonely graveyard of Mont Muret, one looks over a tortured wilderness of trenches and shell-holes. Close by are all the places famous through years of fighting—Souain, Navarin Farm, Tahure, the Butte de Tahure, and, to the north-west, Somme-Py, Ste. Marie-Py, and so on to Moronvilliers and Craonne. In the south-western distance I could just descry the Monts de Champagne, while turning to the north one faced the slopes of Notre Dame des Champs, and recalled the statement of General Gouraud that on that comparatively open ground the fiercest fighting of last October had taken place.

And now, not a soul, not a movement! Everywhere lay piles of unused shell, German and French, small heaps of hand-grenades and bundles of barbed wire. The camouflaged battery positions, the deep dug-outs and strong posts of the enemy were all about us; a dead horse lay not far away; and in front, the white crosses of the graveyard. A grim scene, under the January sky! But in the very middle of the little cemetery some tender hand had just recently fastened a large bunch of white narcissus to one of the crosses. We had passed no one that I could remember on the long ascent; yet the flowers were quite fresh and the thought of them—the only living and beautiful thing for miles in that scarred wilderness, over which a creeping fog was beginning to gather—stayed with me for days.

The Champagne-battle-field is indeed deeply interwoven with the whole history of the war. The flower of the French Army and almost all the leading French Generals—Castelnau, Petain, Nivelle, Gouraud, have passed through its furnace. But famous as it is, and for ever associated with the remarkable and fascinating personality of General Gouraud, which gives to it a *panache* of its own, it has not the sacredness of Verdun.

We had spent the day before the expedition to Champagne at St. Mihiel and Verdun. To St. Mihiel I will return in my next chapter. Verdun I had never seen, and the impression that it makes, even in a few hours, is profound. In March, 1916, I well remember at Havre, at Boulogne, at St. Omer, how intent and absorbed a watch was kept along our front over the news from Verdun. It came in hourly, and the officers in the hotels, French and English, passed it to each other without much speech, with a shrug, or a look of anxiety, or a smile, as the case might be. When we arrived on March 6th at the Visitors' Chateau at G.H.Q.—then, of course, at St. Omer—our first question was: "Verdun?" "All right," was the quick reply. "We have offered help, but they have refused it."

No—France, heroic France, trod that wine-press alone; she beat back her cruel foe alone; and, at Verdun, she triumphed alone. Never, indeed, was human sacrifice more absolute; and never was the spiritual force of what men call patriotism more terribly proved. "The *poilu* of Verdun," writes M. Joseph Reinach, "became an epic figure"—and the whole battle rose before Europe as a kind of apocalyptic vision of Death and Courage, staged on a great river, in an amphitheatre of blood-stained hills. All the eyes in the world were fixed on this little corner of France. For a Frenchman—"Verdun was our first thought on waking, and was never absent from us through the day."

The impression made by the battle—or rather, the three battles—of Verdun does not depend on the numbers engaged. The British Battle of the Somme, and the battles of last year on the British front far surpassed it in the number of men and guns employed. From March 21st last year to April 17th, the British front was attacked by 109 divisions, and the French by 25. In the most critical fighting at Verdun, from February 21st to March 21st, the French had to face 21 divisions, and including the second German attack in June and the triumphant French advance in December, the total enemy forces may be put at 42 divisions. But the story is incomparable! Everything contributed—the fame of the ancient fortress, the dynastic and political interests involved, the passion of patriotism which the struggle evoked in France, the spendthrift waste of life on the part of the German Command.

After the French rally, indeed, from the first terrific bombardment, which nearly gave the German Command its coveted prey, the thing became a duel, watched by all Europe, between Petain and the Crown Prince; between the dynastic interests of the Hohenzollerns, served by a magnificent army, and the finest military and patriotic traditions of France. From day to day the public in this country watched the fluctuations of the struggle with an interest so absorbing that the names of Douaumont, Vaux, Mort Homme, Cumieres, the Goose's Crest, came to ring in our ears almost as the names of Hougoumont, La Haye Sainte, La Belle Alliance, rang in those of an earlier time.

Verdun, from a distance, produces the same illusion as Rheims. The Cathedral and the town are apparently still in being. They have not lost their essential outlines, and the veils of grey and purple haze between the spectator and the reality disguises what both have suffered. Then one draws nearer. One enters the famous fortress, through the old Vauban fortifications, and over the Vauban bridge—little touched, to all appearance. And presently, as one passes along the streets, one sees that here is not a town, but only the ghost, the skeleton of a town. The roofless, windowless houses, of which the streets still keep, as in Rheims, their ancient lines, stare at you like so many eyeless skulls—the bare bones of a city. Only the famous citadel, with its miles of underground passages and rooms, is just as it was before the battle, and as it will be, one may hope, through the long years to come; preserved, not for any active purpose of war, but as the shrine of immortal memories. Itself, it played a great part in the struggle. For here, in these dormitories and mess-rooms and passages so far underground that even the noise of the fierce struggle outside never reached them, it was possible for troops worn out by the superhuman ordeal of the battle, to find complete rest—*to sleep*—without fear.

We entered through a large mess-room full of soldiers, with, at its further end, a kitchen, with a busy array of cooks and orderlies. Then someone opened a door, and we found ourselves in a small room, very famous in the history of the war. During the siege, scores of visitors from Allied and neutral countries—statesmen, generals, crowned heads—took luncheon under its canopy of flags, buried deep underground, while the storm of shell raged outside. There, in the visitors' book, one might turn to the two signatures—one of them then only a fortnight old—that all France knows:

"March, 1916—*On les aura! Petain*"

"January, 1918—*On les a! Petain*"

A courteous Commandant, telephoned to from below, came from some upper region to greet us and to show us something of the endless labyrinth of rooms, passages and dormitories, which during the siege often sheltered thousands of men. The veteran Colonel Duhay, who was in command of the citadel during the greater part of the year-long battle—a splendid, square-built tower of a man—I saw later in Paris. It was ill-luck not to have been able to walk with him over the tragic battle-field itself, for few men can have memories of it at once so comprehensive and so close. From the few words I had with him I retain a shuddering impression as of a slaughter-house; yet nothing could be cheerfuller or humaner than the broad soldier-face. But our talk turned on the losses of Verdun, and although these losses—*i.e.*, the proportion of death to the square yard—were probably exceeded in several later battles, in none, it seems to me, has the massacre of men on both sides left so terrible a mark on the survivors. There came a time when the French were sick of slaying, and the German dead were piled metres high on the slopes of Mort Homme and Cumieres; in those weeks at the end of May, when the Germans, conscious that their prestige had suffered irreparably in the hundred days—which were to have been four!—of desperate and indecisive fighting, were at the opening of that fierce last effort which gave them Fort Vaux and its hero-commander, Commandant Raynal, on June 7th—put them in short-lived possession of Thiaumont and Fleury later—and was then interrupted at the end of the month by the thunder of the Allied attack on the Somme.

After leaving the citadel and the much-injured cathedral, beneath the crypt of which some of the labyrinthine passages of the old fortress are hewn, we drove through the eastern section of the battle-field, past what was once Fort Souville, along an upper road, with Vaux on our right, and Douaumont on the northern edge of the hill in front of us; descending again by Froide Terre, with the Cote de Poivre beyond it to the north; while we looked across the Meuse at the dim lines of Mort Homme, of the Bois des Corbeaux and the Crete de l'Oie, of all that "chess-board" of hills which became so familiar to Europe in those marvellous four months from February to June, 1916. Every yard of these high slopes has been fought over again and again, witnessing on the part of the defenders a fury of endurance, a passion of resolve, such as those, perhaps, alone can know who hear through all their being the mystic call of the soil, of the very earth itself, the actual fatherland, on which they fight. "*We are but a moment of the eternal France*:"—such was once the saying of a French soldier, dying somewhere amid these broken trenches over which we are looking. What was it, asks M. Reinach, that enabled the French to hold out as they did? *Daring*, he replies—the daring of the leaders, the daring of the troops led. The word hardly renders the French "*audace*" which is equally mis-translated by our English "audacity." "*Audace*" implies a daring which is not rashness, a daring which is justified, which is, in fact, the military aspect of a great nation's confidence in itself. It was the spirit of the "Marseillaise," says M. Reinach again—it was the French soul—*l'ame francaise*—the soul of country and of freedom, which triumphed here.

And not for France alone. At the moment when the attack on Verdun began, although the British military power was strengthening month by month, and the Military Service Act of May, 1916, which put the finishing touch to Lord Kitchener's great work, was close at hand, the French Army was still not only the principal, but the essential element in the Western campaign. France, at Verdun, as in the Battle of the Marne, was defending not only her own freedom, but the freedom of Europe. A few months later, when the British Army of the Somme went over its parapets at daybreak on July 1st, Verdun was automatically relieved, and it was clear to all the world that Britain's apprenticeship was past, and that another great military power had been born into Europe, on whom, as we now know, the main responsibilities of final victory were to rest. But at Verdun France fought for *us*—for England and America no less than for herself; and that thought must always deepen the already deep emotion with which English eyes look out upon these tortured hills.

That dim line on the eastern ridge, which marks the ruins of Fort Vaux, stands indeed for a story which has been entrusted by history to the living memory of France's Allies, hardly less than to that of France herself. As we pause among the crumbling trenches and shell-holes to look back upon the height of Vaux, I seem to see the lines of French infantry creeping up the hill, through the communication trenches, in the dark, to the relief of their comrades in the fort; the runners —eager volunteers—assuring communications under the incessant hail of shell; the carrier-pigeons, when the fort is altogether cut off, bringing their messages back to Head-quarters; the red and green signal lights shooting up from the ridge into the night. One of these runners, when the siege was nearing its end, arrived at an advance post, having by a miracle got through a terrible barrage unhurt. "You might have waited a few instants," said the Colonel, kindly. But the runner, astonished, showed the envelope. "My Colonel, look—it is written—'*urgent!*'"

That was the spirit. Or listen to this fragment from the journal of Captain Delvert, defending one of the redoubts that protect Fort Vaux:

"Six o'clock—the bombardment has just begun again. The stretcher-bearer, L—, has just been leaning a few moments —worn out—against the wall of my dug-out. His good, honest face is hollow, his eyes, with their blue rims, seem starting out of his head. '*Mon Capitaine*, I'm used up. There are only three stretcher-bearers left. The others are dead or wounded. I haven't eaten for three days, or drunk a drop of water.' His frail body is only held together by a miracle of energy. Talk of heroes—here is a true one!

"Eight o'clock. We are relieved.

"Eleven o'clock. Message from the Colonel. 'Owing to circumstances the 101st cannot be relieved.'

"*Merci!*

"What a disappointment for my poor fellows! Lieutenant X—is lost in admiration of them. I daresay—but I have only thirty-nine of them left."

Eighteen hours later.

"The order for relief has come. We shall leave our dead behind us in the trench. Then-comrades have carefully placed them out of the passage-way.... There they are—poor sentinels, whom we leave behind us, in a line on the parados, in their blood-stained uniforms—solemn and terrible guardians of this fragment of French soil, which still in death they seem to be holding against the enemy."

But the enemy advances inexorably, and within the fort the dead and dying multiply.

"Captain Tabourot fought like a lion," says another witness. "He was taller than any of us. He gave his orders briefly, encouraged us, and placed us. Then he plunged his hand into the bag of bombs, and, leaning back, threw one with a full swing of the arm, aiming each time. That excited us, and we did our best."

But meanwhile the enemy is stealing up behind, between the trench and the fort. Captain Tabourot is mortally hit, and is carried into the dressing-station within the fort. Commandant Raynal, himself wounded, comes to see him. "No word of consolation, no false hope. The one knows that all is over; the other respects him too deeply to attempt a falsehood." A grasp of the hand—a word from the Commandant: "Well done, *mon ami*!" But the Captain is thinking of his men. "*Mon Commandant*—if the Boches get through, it is not the fault of my company. They did all they could." Then a last message to his wife. And presently his name is carried through the dark by a carrier-pigeon down to the Headquarters below: "The enemy surrounds us. I report to you the bravery of Captain Tabourot, seriously wounded. We are holding out." And a few hours later: "Captain Tabourot of the 142nd has died gloriously. Wound received in defending the north-eastern breach. Demand for him the Legion of Honour."

For five days the heroic defence goes on. All communications are cut, the passages of the fort are choked with wounded and dying men, the water is giving out. On the 4th, a wounded pigeon arrives at Headquarters. It brings a message, imploring urgently for help.

"This is my last pigeon." The following day communication is partly re-established, and a few fragmentary messages are received. "The enemy"—signals the fort—"is working on a mine to the west of the fort. Turn on the guns—quick." ... "We don't hear your artillery. Are attacked by gas, and flame throwers. Are at the last extremity." Then one message gets through from below—"Courage! we shall soon attack." The fort waits, and at night another fragmentary message comes from Raynal asking for water and relief. "I am nearly at the end of my powers. The troops—men and officers—have in all circumstances done their duty.... You will come, no doubt ... before we are completely exhausted. *Vive la France!*"

But death and thirst—thirst, above all—are victors. On the 6th, a few hours before the inevitable end, Marshal Joffre flashed his message to the heights—in the first place, a message of thanks to troops and Commander for their "magnificent defence," in the next, making Commandant Raynal a Commander of the Legion of Honour.

On the 7th a last heroic effort was made to relieve the fort. It failed, and Raynal—wounded, with a handful of survivors—surrendered, the Germans, in acknowledgment of the heroism of the defence, allowing the Commandant to retain his sword.

What manner of men were they that fought this fight? What traditions did they represent? What homes did they come from?

M. Henri Bordeaux, himself an eye-witness, to whose admirable and moving book on *The Last Days of Fort Vaux*, I am indebted for the preceding details, to some extent answers the question by quoting a letter, addressed by his mother to the stretcher-bearer, Roger Vamier, decorated in 1915 by General Joffre himself.

> "*Et toi, mon tresor*—you must have a great deal to do.... Well, do all you can to save those poor wounded!—left there in the snow and blood. My blood boils to be staying on here, when there is so much to do over there, in picking up those poor fellows. Why won't they have a woman? —there, where she could really help! It is the business of mothers to pick up those poor lads, and give them a good word. Well, you must replace the mothers, you, *mon cheri*, you must do all you can—do the impossible—to help. I see you running—creeping along—looking for the wounded. If I could only be there too!—Yes, it is my place, *mon petit*, near you. Courage, courage!—I know it is the beginning of the end—and the end will be grand for all those who have fought in the just cause."

A month later thousands of English, Scotch, Welsh and Irish lads, men from Canada, South Africa, New Zealand, and Australia, were passing on the Somme through a similar furnace of death and suffering to that borne by the French at Verdun. But the English ways of expression are not the French; and both differ from the American. The instinct for ringing and dramatic speech rarely deserts the Frenchman—or Frenchwoman. It is present in the letter written by Roger Vamier's mother, as in the *Ordres du Jour* of Castelnau or

Petain. Facility of this kind is not our *forte*. Our lack of it suggests the laughter in that most delightful of recent French books, *Les Silences du Colonel Bramble*, which turns upon our national taciturnities and our minimising instinct in any matter of feeling, an instinct which is like the hiding instinct, the protective colouring of birds—only anxious to be mistaken for something else. The Englishman, when emotion compels him, speaks more readily in poetry than prose; it is the natural result of our great poetic tradition; and in the remarkable collections of war poetry written by English soldiers we have the English counterpart to the French prose utterance of the war—so much more eloquent and effective, generally, than our own.

*   *   *   *   *

One more look round the slopes over which the light is fading. The heroism of the defence!—that, here, is the first thought. But on the part of the attackers there was a courage no less amazing, though of another sort; the effect of an iron discipline hypnotising the individual will, and conferring on the soldier such superhuman power of dying at another man's will as history—on such a scale—has scarcely seen equalled. In the first battle of Verdun, which lasted forty-eight days (February 21st to April 9th), the German casualties were over 200,000, with a very high proportion of killed. And by the end of the year the casualties at Verdun, on both sides, had reached 700,000. Opinion in Germany, at first so confident, wavered and dropped. Why not break off? But the dynasty was concerned. Fortune, *toute entiere a sa proie attachee*, drove the German Army again and again through lanes of death, where the French 75's worked their terrible will—for no real military advantage. "On the 10th of March," says M. Henri Bordeaux, "the enemy climbed the northern slopes of Fort Vaux. He was then from two to three hundred metres from the counter-scarp. He took three months to cross these two to three hundred metres—three months of superhuman effort, and of incredible losses in young men, the flower of the nation." The German strategic reserves were for the first time seriously shaken, and by the end of this wonderful year Petain, Nivelle, and Mangin between them had recovered from the assailants all but a fraction of what had been lost at Verdun. Meanwhile, behind the "shield" of Verdun, which was thus attracting and wasting the force of the enemy, the Allied Armies had prepared the great offensive of the summer. Italy struck in the Trentino on the 25th of June, Russia attacked in June and July, the British attacked on the Somme on July 1st. The "wearing-down" battle had begun in earnest. "Soldiers of Verdun," said Marshal Joffre, in his order of the 12th of June, "the plans determined on by the Coalition are in full work. It is your heroic resistance that has made this possible. It was the indispensable condition, and it will be the foundation, of our coming victories." "Germany"—says M. Reinach—"during ten months had used her best soldiers in furious assaults on Verdun.... These troops, among the finest in the world, had in five of these months gained a few kilometres of ground on the road to the fortress. This ground, watered with blood as no field of carnage had ever been, which saw close upon 700,000 men fall, was lost in two actions (October 24th—November 3rd and December 15th—18th), and Germany was brought back to within a few furlongs of her starting point.... Douaumont and Louvemont were certainly neither Rocroy nor Austerlitz; but Verdun, from the first day to the last, from the rush stemmed by Castelnau to the battles won by Nivelle and Mangin; Verdun, with her mud-stained *poilu*, standing firm in the tempest, who said: "They shall not pass!" *(passeront pas!)*, and they have not passed; Verdun, for the Germans a charnel-house, for us a sanctuary, was something greater by far."

With these thoughts in mind we dropped down the long hill to Verdun again, and so across the bridge and on to that famous road, the *Voie Sacree*, up which Petain, "the road-mender" (*Le Cantonnier*), brought all his supplies—men, food, guns, ammunition—from Bar-le-Duc by motor-lorry, passing and repassing each other in a perpetual succession—one every twenty seconds. The road was endlessly broken up, sometimes by the traffic, sometimes by shell, and as endlessly repaired by troops specially assigned to the task. And presently we are passing the Moulin des Regrets, where Castelnau and Petain met on the night of the 25th, and the resolution was taken to counter-attack instead of withdrawing. Verdun, indeed, is the classic illustration of the maxim that attack is the best defence, or, as the British Commander-in-Chief puts it in his latest dispatch, that "defensive success in battle can be gained only by a vigorous offensive." The long battle on the Meuse, "the greatest single action in history," was in one aspect a vast school, in which a score of matters belonging to the art of war were tested, illustrated, and explained, with the same general result as appears throughout the struggle, a result insisted on by each great commander, British or French, in turn; *i.e.*, that in the principles of war there is nothing new to be learnt. Discipline, training, co-operation, attack; these are the unchanging forces the great general has at command. It depends on his own genius what he makes of them.

Verdun fades behind us, and we are on our way to the Marne. In the strange isolation of the car, passing so quickly, as the short winter twilight comes on, through country one has never seen before and will perhaps never see again, the war becomes a living pageant on the background of the dark. Then, with the lights of Chateau-Thierry, thought jumps in a moment from the oldest army in the war to the youngest. This old town, these dim banks of the Marne, have a long history. But in the history of last year, and the closing scenes of the Great War, they belong specially to America. This is American ground.

To realise what that means, we must retrace our steps a little.

CHAPTER VI

AMERICA IN FRANCE

On March 2nd, 1917, I found myself lunching at Montreuil, then the General Headquarters of the British Expeditionary Force, with the Staff of the Intelligence Department. After lunch I walked through the interesting old town, with the Chief of the Department, and our talk turned on the two subjects of supreme importance at that moment—America and Russia. When would America come in? For that she would come in was clear. It was now a full month since diplomatic relations between Germany and the United States had been broken off, and about a week since President Wilson had asked Congress to arm American vessels in self-defence against the new submarine campaign announced by Germany in January. "It can't be long," said my companion quietly; "Germany has gone too far to draw back. And the President will have the whole country with him. On the whole I think he has been right to wait. It is from Americans themselves of course that one hears the sharpest criticism of the President's 'patience.'"

My own correspondence of the winter indeed with American friends had shown me the passion of that criticism. But on the 2nd of March there was small further need for it. Germany was rushing on her fate. During the course of the month, England and America watched the piling up of the German score as vessel after vessel was sunk. Then on the 1st of April came the loss of twenty-eight American lives in the *Aztec*, and the next day but one we opened our London newspapers to find that on

April the 2nd President Wilson had asked Congress for a Declaration of War.

"America is in," wrote an officer at G.H.Q., "and the faces of everybody one sees show a real bit of spring sunshine. People begin to say: 'Now we shall be home by Christmas.'"

But something else had happened in that fateful month of March. March the 9th saw the strange, uncertain opening of the Russian revolution, followed by a burst of sympathy and rejoicing throughout Europe. Only those intimately acquainted with the structure of Russian society felt the misgivings of those who see the fall of a house built on rotten foundations and have no certainty of any firm ground whereon to build its successor. But the disappointment and exasperation of the Allies at that moment, as to all that had happened in Russia during the preceding months, under the old regime, was so great that the mere change bred hope; and for a long time we hoped against hope. All the more because the entry of America, and the thrilling rapidity of her earlier action put the Russian business into the shade, may, indeed, have dulled the perceptions of the Allies with regard to it. In forty days from the declaration of war the United States had adopted Conscription, which had taken us two years; General Pershing and his small force had sailed for France within eighty days; and by the end of June, or within ninety days, America had adopted the blockade policy of Great Britain, and assented to the full use of that mighty weapon which was to have so vast an influence on the war. President Wilson's speech, when he came to Congress for the Declaration of War, revealed him— and America—to England, then sorely brooding over "too proud to fight," in an aspect which revived in us all that was kinship and sympathy, and put to sleep the natural resentments and astonishments of the preceding years. Nay, we envied America a man capable of giving such magnificent expression to the passion and determination of all free nations, in face of the German challenge.

Then came the days of disappointment. Troops arrived at a

more leisurely pace in France than had been hoped. Ships and aeroplanes, which American enthusiasm in the early weeks of the war had promised in profusion, delayed their coming; there was congestion on the American railways, interfering with supplies of all kinds; and the Weather God, besides, let loose all his storm and snow battalions upon the Northern States to hamper the work of transport. We in England watched these things, not realising that our own confidence in the military prospects and the resisting power of the Allies, was partly to blame for American leisureliness. It was so natural that American opinion, watching the war, should split into two phases—one that held the war was going to be won quickly by negotiation, before America could seriously come in; the other that the war would go on for another three years, and therefore there would be ample time for America to make all her own independent plans and form her own separate army with purely American equipment. English opinion wavered in the same way. I well remember a gathering in a London house in November, 1917, just after the first successful attack in the Battle of Cambrai. It was a gathering in honour of General Bliss, and other American officers and high officials then in London. General Bliss was the centre of it, and the rugged, most human, most lovable figure of Mr. Page was not far away. The Battle of Cambrai was in progress, and English expectations, terribly depressed, at any rate among those who knew, by the reports which had been coming through of the severe fighting in the Salient, during the preceding weeks, were again rising rapidly. Everybody was full of the success of the initial attack, of the tanks above all, and what they might mean for the future. At last Sir Julian Byng had achieved surprise; at last there had been open fighting; if by happy chance we took Cambrai what might not happen? A flash of optimism ran through us all. Victory and peace drew nearer. Yet in the background there were always those dim rumours of the appalling losses at Passchendaele, together with the smarting memory of Caporetto, and of the British divisions sent to Italy.

And in ten days more we knew that the German counter-attack had checked the Cambrai advance, that Bourlon Wood was lost, that Cambrai was still inaccessible, and we retained only a portion of the ground gained by the dash and skill of the first days. The moral was, as always—"more men!" and we settled down again to a stubborn waiting for our own new recruits, then in the training camps, and for the first appearance of the American battalions. Meanwhile the news from Russia grew steadily worse; the Russian Army had melted away under the Kerensky regulations; and the country was rapidly falling into chaos. Brest-Litovsk was acutely realised for the German triumph that it was; and the heads of the Army were already calculating with some precision the number of German divisions, then on the Eastern front, which must inevitably be transferred to France for the spring offensive of the German Army.

It was natural that those really acquainted with the situation should turn feverishly towards America. When was her Army coming? In the matter of money America had done nobly towards all the Allies. In this field her help had been incalculably great. In the matter of munitions and stores for the Allies she had done all that the state of her railways, the weather of her winter, and the drawbacks of the American Constitution, considered as a military machine, as yet allowed her to do. Meanwhile one saw the President, aided by a score of able and energetic men, constantly at work removing stones in the path, setting up a War Industries Board, reorganising the Shipping Board and the Air Service, and clearing the way for those food supplies from the great American and Canadian wheatfields without which Europe could not endure, and which were constantly endangered by the pressure of the submarine attack. Perhaps in all that anxious winter the phase of American help which touched us English folk most deeply was the voluntary rationing by which hundreds and thousands of American families, all over the vast area of the States, eagerly stinted themselves that they might send food overseas to Great Britain and the Allies—sixty million bushels of wheat by January 1st—ninety millions before the 1918 harvest. We knew that it was only done by personal sacrifice, and we *felt* it in our hearts.

Meanwhile, on this side of the sea, the anxiety for *men* grew steadily stronger. Who knew what the coming spring campaign would bring forth? The French Army during 1917 had passed through that *depression morale* of which I have spoken in an earlier letter. Would a country which had borne such a long and terrible ordeal of death and devastation be capable of yet another great effort during the coming year, whatever might be the heroic patriotism of her people? One heard of the enormous preparations that America was making in France—of the new docks, warehouses, and railways, of the vast depots and splendid camps that were being laid out—with a mixture of wonder and irritation. A friend of mine, on coming back from France, described to me his going over a new American dock with two French officers: "Magnificent!" said the Frenchmen, in a kind of despair—"but when are they going to *begin*? Suppose the war is over, and France swallowed up, *before* they begin?" A large section of American opinion was shaken with the same impatience.

American letters to English friends, including those of Mr. Roosevelt to his many English correspondents, among whom, to some small extent, I was proud to reckon myself, expressed an almost fierce disappointment with the slow progress of things. Ultimately, of course, an independent American Army, under its own Commander-in-Chief, and fully equipped from American factories. But why not begin by sending men in as large numbers as possible to train with the British and French Armies, and to take their places as soon as possible in the fighting line, as integral parts of those armies, allowing the Allies to furnish all equipment till America was really ready? It was pointed out that Canada and Australia, by sending officers and men over at once to train and fight with the British, and leaving everything else to be supplied by the Allies, had in nine months from the outbreak of war already taken part in glorious and decisive battles. Or why not adopt a two-fold policy—of supplying men to the Allies as rapidly as possible, for immediate aid, carrying on preparations the while for an independent American Army with all its own supplies, as the ultimate goal? Time, it was urged, was of the utmost importance. And what object was served by experimenting with new types of munitions, instead of adopting the types of the Allies, which the American factories were already turning out in profusion? And so on.

With such feelings did many of us on this side of the water, and a large section apparently of American friends of the Allies on the other side, watch the gradual unravelling of America's tangled skeins. The *North American Review* asked in December, 1917: "Are we losing the war? No. But we are not winning it." In January, 1918, the editor warned his readers: "The Allied forces are not in condition to withstand the terrific onslaught which Germany is bound to make within six months. America must win the war." In April the *New York Bankers' Bulletin* said: "We have not made progress as far as we might or could," while months later, even in its September number (1918), the *North American Review* still talked of "our inexplicable military sluggishness," and rang with appeals for greater energy. There was of course an element of politics in all this; but up to March last year it is clear that, in spite of many things not only magnificently planned, but magnificently *done*, there was a great deal of sincere anxiety and misgiving in both countries.

But with the outbreak of the German offensive in March, as we all know, everything changed. American troops began to *rush* over:—366,000 in round numbers, up to the end of March, and 440,000 more, up to the end of June, 70 per cent, of them carried in British ships; a million by the end of July, nearly a million and a half before the Armistice. Wonderful story! Nobody, I think, can possibly exaggerate the heartening and cheering effect of it upon the Allies in Europe, especially on France—wounded and devastated France—and on Italy, painfully recovering from Caporetto. How well I remember the thrill of those days in London, the rumours of the weekly landings of troops—70,000—80,000 men—and the occasional sight of the lithe, straight-limbed, American boys marching through our streets!

And yet, curiously enough—what *was* exaggerated all the time, on both sides of the Atlantic, both here and in America, was the extent of the British set-back hi March and April, and its effect on the general situation. That is clear, I think, when we look back on our own Press at home, and still more on American utterances, both in the States and in France. In *August* of last year Mr. Secretary Baker said: "We are only just beginning"—and he pointed to the millions of men that America would have in France by 1919. On August 7th General March, Chief of the American General Staff, said in the Senate Committee, that America would have four millions of men in France, with one million at home, for the campaign of 1919. "The only way that Germany can be whipped is by America going into this thing with her whole strength. It is up to us to win the war.... We must force the issue and win." The editor of the *North American Review* wrote in August, and published in his September number, phrases like the following: "But the hand of the enemy cannot be struck down for a long time to come." "Virtually impregnable positions" are still held by him. "No military observer is so sanguine as to anticipate anything like conclusive results from the present campaign. The real test will come next year, in the late spring and summer of 1919." By then the Allies must have "a great preponderance of men and guns. These America must supply."

But when General March said in August: "It is up to us to win the war," and the *North American Review* talked of "virtually impregnable positions," and the impossibility of "anything like conclusive results from the present campaign"—the capture of those "impregnable positions" by the British Army, and thereby the winning of the war, were only a few weeks away! Similar phrases could be quoted from the British Press, and from prominent Englishmen, though not, unless my memory plays me false, from any of our responsible military leaders. The fact is that the view I represented, in my second article, as the view taken by the heads of the British Army, of the March retreat, had turned out by the summer to be the true one. The German armies *had* to a large extent beaten themselves out against the British defensive battle of the spring: and while the

Americans were making their splendid spurt from April to August, and entering the fighting field in force for the first time, the British Army, having absorbed its recruits, taken huge toll of its enemies, and profited by all there was to be learnt from the German offensive, was getting ready every day to give the final strokes in the war, aided, when the moment came, by the supreme leadership of Marshal Foch, by the successes of Generals Mangin and Degoutte on the Marne, by the masterly campaign of General Gouraud in Champagne, and the gallant push of General Pershing in the Argonne. This position of things was not sufficiently realised by the general public in England, still less by the American public, as is shown by the extracts I have quoted. So that the continuous series of British victories, from August 8th onward, which ended in the Armistice, came as a rather startling surprise to those both here and abroad who, like von Kluck in 1914, had been inclined to make too much of a temporary British retreat.

Moreover, behind the military successes of Great Britain—and not only on the French front, but in the East also—stood always the deadly pressure of the British blockade. When after the capture of the Hindenburg positions, the line indicating "prisoners," on that chart at G.H.Q., a reduced copy of which will be found at the end of this book, leapt up to a height for which the wall in the room of the Director of Operations could hardly find space, it meant not only victory over Germany in the field, but also the disintegration of German *morale* at home; owing first and foremost to that deadly watch which the British Navy, supported during the last year of the war by the American embargo, had kept over the seas of the world, to Germany's undoing, since the opening of the struggle. The final victory of the Allies when it came was thus in a special sense Great Britain's victory, achieved both by her mastery of the sea, and the military expansion forced upon her by the German attack; conditioned, of course, by the whole earlier history of the war, in which France had led the van and borne the brunt, and immensely facilitated by the "splendid American adventure," to use the phrase of an American.

For to show that, in a strictly military sense, the British and Dominion Armies, backed by the British Navy, brought the war to a successful end—a simple matter of figures and dates—is not all, or nearly all. The American intervention, and especially the marvellous speeding-up of American action, from March to the end of the war, quite apart from the brilliant promise of America's first appearances in the field, had an effect upon Europe—Great Britain, France, Italy—akin to that which the American climate and atmosphere produces on the visitor from this side of the Atlantic. It breathed new life into everything, and especially into the heart of France, the chief sufferer by three years of atrocious war. As weary and devastated France watched the American stream of eager and high-hearted youth, flowing from Bordeaux eastwards, column after column, regiment after regiment, of men admirable in physique, fearless in danger, and full of a laughing and boundless confidence in America's power to help, and resolve to win—at last it seemed that the long horror of the war must be indeed coming to an end. "Three thousand miles!" said the French villager or townsman to himself, as he turned out to see them pass—"they have come three thousand miles to beat the Boche. And America is the richest country in the world—and there are a hundred millions of them." Hope rose into flood, and with it fresh courage to endure.

Nor was the effect less marked on the British nation, which had not known invasion, and on the British Army, for all its faith in itself. The rapid growth of American strength in France from March onward in response to the call of the Allies, provided indeed a moral support to the two older armies, which was of incalculable value and "influenced the fighting qualities of both; while the knowledge of these mounting reserves enabled the Allied Commanders to take risks which otherwise could hardly have been faced." I am quoting a British military authority of high rank.

It was at Metz that—outside Paris—I first came in contact with this "America in France," which History will mark on her coming page with all the emphasis that belongs to new chapters in the ever-broadening tale of man. It was in the shape of some "Knights of Columbus," pausing at Metz for a night on their way to Coblenz. We only exchanged a few words on the steps of the hotel, but I had time to feel the interest and the strangeness of this American Catholicism in Europe, following in the track of war, and looking with its New World eyes at those old, old towns, those ancient churches in which American Catholics were at home, yet not at home. At Strasbourg I saw no Americans that I can remember. But our arrival at Nancy at midnight, very weary after a long day in the car, during which we had missed our way badly at least once, is linked in my recollection with the apparition of two young American officers just as we were being told for the third time that there was no room in the hotel to which we had driven up. Should we really have to sleep in the car? There seemed to be not a single vacant bedroom in Nancy; and there had been snow showers during the day! But these two Americans heard from our French Lieutenant that there were two English ladies in the car, and they came forward at once, offering their rooms. Luckily we found shelter elsewhere; but I shall not soon forget the kind readiness of the two young men, and the thrill of the whole scene. There we stood in the beautiful Place Stanislas, that workmen from Versailles built for the father-in-law of Louis Quinze. A flickering moonlight touched the gilding of the famous *grilles* that shut in the square; and the only light in the wide space seemed to come from this one hotel taken by the American authorities for the use of their officers and Red Cross workers passing to and from the Rhine. When that square was built, George Washington was a youth of twenty, and after one hundred and seventy years it stood within the war-zone of an American Army, which had crossed the Atlantic to fight in Europe!

Next day we spent entirely in the American sector, between Nancy and Toul, where American road directions and sign-boards, and fine, newly-built camps and depots for the American forces met us in all directions. A military policeman from a coloured regiment put us into the right road for St.

Mihiel after leaving Toul—a strongly-built, bronzed fellow, dealing with the stream of military and civil traffic at a cross roads in Eastern France with perfect ease and *sang-froid*. The astonishment and interest of this American occupation of a country so intensely and ultimately national, so little concerned in ordinary times with any other life than its own as France, provincial France above all, never ceased to hold me as we drove on and on through the American sector; especially when darkness and moonlight returned, and again and again as we passed through wrecked villages where a few chinks of light here and there showed a scattered billet or two, the American military policeman on duty would emerge from the shadows, tall, courteous, self-possessed, to answer a question, or show the way, and we left him behind, apparently the only human being under the French night, in sole possession of the ruins round him.

But before darkness fell, during the central part of the day, we had crossed the southern lines of the convergent American attack on St. Mihiel. Trenches and wire-fields and artillery positions had all belonged to the French battle-zone before the Americans took them over, and there had been fierce fighting here by the French in 1915. But for three years the position had changed but little, till the newly-formed First American Army undertook in September the clearing of the Salient.

We left the car near the village of Beaumont, and walked to the brow of the low ridge from which the American attack started. Standing among what had been the *tranckees de depart*, with the ruins of the village of Seichprey below us to the right, we had before us the greater part of the American battle-field—Thiaucourt in the far north-east; the ridge of Vigne-ulles, which had been the meeting-point of the converging American attacks coming both from the north-west and the south-east; while in the near foreground rose the once heavily fortified Mont Sec. The American troops went over the parapet at five o'clock on the morning of September 12th, and by the morning of the 13th their forces had met at Vigneulles, and the Salient, with its perpetual threat to the French line, had disappeared. In three more days the Heights of the Meuse had been cleared, and the foremost Americans were already under the fire of the fortified zone protecting Metz.

It was a brilliant but happily not a costly victory. Von Gallwitz, the German Commander, had probably already determined on retirement, when the American attack forestalled him. So that the American troops with certain French units supporting them achieved a great result with small losses; and as the first battle of an independent American Army the operation must always remain one of extraordinary interest and importance, even though, in British military opinion, the palm of difficulty and of sacrifice must be given rather to the splendid fighting on the Marne in June and July, when the Americans were still under French direction, or to the admirable performance of the two American divisions, the 27th and the 30th, serving under Sir Henry Rawlinson, a fortnight after St. Mihiel, on the Hindenburg line. "The original attack," at St. Mihiel, says one of the keenest of British military observers—"was carried out with extraordinary dash by very eager and physically magnificent soldiers." Possibly, he adds, a more seasoned army—the American troops had only had six months' experience in the fighting line!—might have turned the effects of a successful action to greater military advantage than was the case at St. Mihiel. The British or French critic, mindful of the bitter lessons of four years of war, is inclined to make the same criticism of most of the American operations of last year, except the fighting on the Marne in June and July, when French caution and experience found a wonderful complement in the splendid fighting qualities of the American infantry. "But"—adds one of them—"undoubtedly the American Command was learning *very rapidly*." What an army the American Army would have been, if the war had lasted through this year! The qualities of the individual soldier, drawn many of them from districts among the naturally richest in the world, together with the vast resources in men and wealth of the nation behind them, and the mastery of the lessons of modern war which was already promised by the American Command, during the six months' campaign of

1918—above all, the comparative freshness of the American effort—would, no doubt, have made the United States Army the leading force among the Allies, had the war been prolonged. That is one line of speculation, and an interesting one. Another, less profitable, asks: "Could the Allies have won without America?" The answer I have heard most commonly given is: "Probably yes, considering, especially, the disintegration we now know to have been going on in Germany, and the cumulative effects of the British blockade. But it would have taken at least six months more fighting, the loss of thousands more precious and irreplaceable lives, and the squandering of vast additional wealth in the bottomless waste of war."

Thank God, we did not win without America! The effects, the far-reaching effects, of America's intervention, of her comradeship in the field of suffering and sacrifice with the free nations of old Europe, are only now beginning to show themselves above the horizon. They will be actively and, as at least the men and women of faith among us believe, beneficently at work, when this generation has long passed away.

CHAPTER VII

AMERICA IN FRANCE (CONTINUED)

It was late when we left Verdun, on the afternoon of the day which saw us at its beginning on the southern edge of the St. Mihiel battle-field, and the winter daylight had passed into darkness before we began to run through a corner of the Argonne, on our way to St. Menehould and Chalons, passing by the wholly ruined village of Clermont in Argonne. The forest ran past us, a wintry fairyland, dimly lit by our quickly moving lamps, and apparently impenetrable beyond their range, an optical effect, however, that may be produced in darkness by a mere fringe of trees along the roadside. But I knew while I watched the exquisite effects of brown and silver, produced by the succession of tall, pale trunks rising above the lace-work of the underwood, as scene after scene pressed upon us out of the dark, that we were indeed in a forest country, only some twenty miles away from the scene of General Pershing's drive at the end of last September, when he achieved on the first day an advance of seven miles through difficult country, while General Gouraud was pushing forward in Champagne; and I found myself speculating in the dark on the many discussions I had heard both among English and Americans of that advance, and of the checks and difficulties which, as I suppose is now generally admitted, followed on the first brilliant operations.

During the last few weeks further information has been forthcoming about the Meuse-Argonne battle, as the American operations between the Argonne and the Meuse from September 26th to November 11th are apparently to be known. But a good deal of obscurity still hangs over the details of the fighting. In the British Army I came across the very general belief that the staff and transport work of the advance had been—in the words of a well-known historian of the war—"as was natural with a new army, scarcely adequate to the fighting qualities of the troops engaged." And I often heard regret expressed that the American Command had not been more willing to avail itself of the staff experience of either or both of the older armies, which might—so the British or French spectator thinks—have lessened the casualty lists among extraordinarily gallant but inexperienced troops. "Replacements fresh from home were put into exhausted divisions with little time for training," says General Pershing's report. And "some of the divisions were fighting their first battle." They were faced also at the beginning of the advance by some of the best remaining German troops. When one thinks of all the long and bitter training in the field that went to the perfecting of French or British staff work, and then of the difficult nature of the ground over which the First American Army had to make its way, one can only feel the deepest sympathy for the losses sustained by the fresh and eager troops. The Argonne forest itself had long been recognised as impenetrable to frontal attack, and on the Argonne side of the American twenty-mile front, along the western edge of the valley of the Aire, the ground is still heavily wooded and often very hilly. As one of the ablest military critics, himself a soldier of great distinction, expressed it to me: "Foch had set the Americans an uncommonly hard task!"

But if there was some failure in those matters where neither bravery nor natural intelligence can take the place of long training, and experience in the field, there was no failure in ardour or in spirit. In spite of heavy losses, General Pershing never failed to push on. Starting from a line on the northern edge of the great Verdun battle-field, Montfaucon, the German headquarters during the Verdun fighting of 1916, was captured in three days. Then came severe fighting against fierce counter-attacks, and great difficulties with transport over shell-torn ground and broken roads, difficulties increased by bad weather. But on October 4th the gallant attack was renewed, and by October 10th, owing to the combined effects of the British drive in the north and the pressure on both sides of the Argonne, from General Gouraud on the west and the Americans on the east, the enemy fell back and the famous forest was cleared.

The third and last phase of the fighting began on the 23rd of October. The enemy was now weakening rapidly along the whole of his line. For while the American Army had been stubbornly fighting its way north from Varennes to Grandpre, where it stood on November 1st, the British Armies, in the great Battles of Cambrai-St. Quentin, Ypres, and Courtrai, had not only captured the Hindenburg line and some fifty thousand prisoners, but had brought about—without fighting—the evacuation of Laon and the retreat of the Germans to the line of the Aisne; the German withdrawal, also, to the Scheldt, involving the freeing of Lille and the great industrial district of France; and finally, in concert with Belgian, French, and some American units, the clearing of the Belgian coast, and the recovery of Ostend, Zeebrugge and Bruges. The end, indeed, was rushing on. Co-operation was everywhere maintained, and blow followed blow. "During this period" (6th to 31st October), says the British Commander-in-Chief, "our Allies had been pushing forward steadily on both sides of the Argonne. The enemy was held by their attacks on his southern flank, while to the north the British offensive was driving forward rapidly behind his right."

Then, with November, the British Army, in the Battle of the Sambre, "struck at and broke the enemy's last important lateral communications, divided his forces into two parts on either side of the Ardennes, and initiated a pursuit which only stopped with the Armistice." About one hundred thousand prisoners had been taken by the British Armies since September 26th. "Victory, indeed," in General Gouraud's phrase, "had changed her camp!" Led by her, the British,

French, and American Armies streamed east and north through the few days that remained, pursuing a beaten and demoralised enemy. The final American advance was begun on November 1st, and on November 7th patrols of the 42nd Division reached the Meuse at Wadelincourt, opposite Sedan; while the Fifth Division was in the Forest of Woevre, and the 90th Division had captured Stenay.

Some very interesting figures have lately been given as to the forces under General Pershing's command. Altogether some 770,000 men seem to have been employed—both east and west of the Meuse—of whom 138,000 were French. Forty-six German divisions, amounting, according to the American estimate, to about 350,000 men, opposed the American advance. The casualties are given as 115,000—among them 26,000 killed[8]—for the American troops, and 7,000 for the French. The enemy casualties are estimated at 75,000, and 16,000 prisoners were taken.

[8] According to the latest estimate I have seen.

One incident, relatively unimportant, but wonderfully picturesque, is sure to find a place in the American song and story of the future. It was during the rapid advance of the last days, when the far vision of the Rhine was already beckoning forward the victorious Allies, and giving wings to the feet of youth. On the night of November 3rd, after a successful day, the 9th and 23rd Infantry of the Second Division found themselves in column formation on the road leading north to Beaumont, a small town south of Sedan. The way lay open, and they took it. They marched on and on through the night, throwing out the usual advance guard and flank patrols, but otherwise unprotected. By all the rules of war the brigade should have been cut off. But in this twilight-time—this *Goetterdaemmerung* of the end, conditions were abnormal, and the two regiments marched on through forest country, right through the enemy lines towards the Meuse, for about eight kilometres, capturing machine-gunners asleep at their guns, and rounding up parties of the enemy on the roads, till in the early dawn they reached a farm where German officers were sitting round tables with lights burning—only to spring to their feet in dismay, as the Americans surrounded them. The cold autumn morning—the young bronzed faces emerging from the darkness—the humbled and astonished foe: surely Old and New, Europe and America, were never brought together in a moment more attractive to the story-teller. A touch of romance amid the tragedy and the glory! But how welcome it is!

The full history, however, of the Argonne fighting will probably not be accurately known for some little time to come. No such obscurity hangs over the glorious fighting on the Marne, through the scenes of which I passed both on the railway journey from Paris to Metz, and in motoring from Chalons to Paris on our return. Colonel Frederick Palmer's book[9] gives an account of these operations, which, it seems to me, ought to be universally read in the Allied countries. The crusading courage of whole-hearted youth, the contempt of death and suffering, the splendid and tireless energy which his pages describe, if they touch other English hearts as deeply as they have touched mine, will go a long way towards that spiritual bond between our nations which alone can make real and lasting things out of Leagues and Treaties.

[9] *America in France*, by Lt.-Col. Frederick Palmer, S.C., U.S.A.

It was on our way from Rheims to Paris after our drive through the Champagne battle-field that we passed rapidly through the places and scenes which Colonel Palmer describes.

As we approached Rheims about midday, a thick white fog rolled suddenly and silently over the chalk uplands that saw General Gouraud's campaign of last September and October. We ran through it, past a turning to Moronvilliers on the left—famous name!—and within a short distance of Nogent l'Abbesse, the fort which did most to wreck Rheims Cathedral, and so down in a dreary semi-darkness into Rheims itself.

Thirty-five years ago I was in Rheims for the first and only time, before this visit. It was in September, not long before the vintage. The town and the country-side were steeped in sunlight, and in the golden riches of Mother Earth. The air indeed, as it shimmered in the heat above the old town, and the hill slopes where the famous vineyards lie, seemed to "drop fatness." Wealth, wine, the body and its pleasures, the cunning handicraft and inherited lore of hundreds of years and many generations seemed to take visible shape in the fine old town, in its vast wine-cellars, and in the old inn where we stayed with its Gargantuan bill of fare, and its *abonnes* from the town, ruddy, full-fleshed citizens, whose achievements in the way of eating and drinking we watched with amazement. Even the cathedral seemed to me to breathe the richness and gaiety of this central France; the sculptures of the facade with its famous "laughing angel" expressed rather the joy of living, of fair womanhood, of smiling maternity, and childhood, of the prime of youth and the satisfied dignity of age, than those austerer lessons of Christianity which speak from Beauvais, or Chartres or Rouen. But how beautiful it all was, how full, wherever one looked, of that old spell of *la douce France*! And now! Under the pall of the fog we drove through the silent ruin of the streets, still on their feet, so to speak, as at Verdun, but eyeless, roofless, and dead, scarcely a house habitable, though here and there one saw a few signs of patching up and returning habitation. And in the great square before the Cathedral instead of the old comeliness, the old stir of provincial and commercial life—*ruin!*—only intensified by a group of motors, come to bring distinguished Sunday visitors from Paris and the Conference, to see as much of it as an hour's wait would enable them to see. There in front of the great portal stood the Prime Minister of England and the Cardinal-Archbishop—heroic Cardinal Lucon, who, under the daily hail of fire, had never left his church or his flock so long as there was a flock in Rheims to shepherd. And above the figure of the Cardinal soared the great West Front, blackened and scarred by fire, the summits of the towers lost in mist, and behind them, the wrecked and roofless church.

The destruction of irreplaceable values, other than human life, caused by the war, is summed up, as far as France is concerned, in this West Front of Rheims; so marred in all its beautiful detail, whether of glass or sculpture, yet still so grand, so instinct still with the pleading powers of the spirit. The "pity of it!" and at the same time, the tenacious undying life of France—all the long past behind her, the unconquerable future before her—these are the ideas one carries away from Rheims, hot in the heart. Above all, for the moment, the pity of it—the horror of this huge outrage spreading from the North Sea to Switzerland, of what the French call so poignantly *nos mines*—symbolised, once for all, by the brutal fate of this poem in stone, built up by the French generations, which is Rheims Cathedral. And as we passed away from Rheims, through the country roads and the bombarded villages of the Tardenois, another district of old France, which up to May last year was still intact, with all its farms and village and country houses, and is now but little different from Artois and Picardy, I found myself thinking with a passionate anxiety, almost, of the Conference sitting in Paris and of its procedure. "France is right—is *right*," I caught myself saying for the hundredth time. "Before anything else—justice to her! —protection and healing for her! Justice on the criminal nation, that has ravaged and trampled on her, 'like a wild beast out of the wood,' and healing for wounds and sufferings that no one can realise who has not witnessed for himself the state of her richest provinces. It was she who offered her breast to the first onslaught of the enemy, she who fought for us all when others had still their armies to make, she who has endured most and bled most, heavily as others—Britain, Italy, Belgium, Serbia—have endured. Her claim must come first— and let those in England and America who wish to realise why *come and see*."

We drove down diagonally through the Marne salient as it was last summer after the German break-through on the Marne, to Dormans and so across the river. In the darkening afternoon we passed over the Montagne de Rheims, and crossed the valley of the Ardre, near the spot where the 19th British

Division, in the German attack of last June, put up so splendid a fight in defence of an important position commanding the valley—the Montagne de Bligny—that the General of the Fifth French Army, General de Mitry, under whose orders they were, wrote to General Haig: "They have enabled us to establish a barrier against which the hostile waves have beaten and shattered themselves. This none of the French who witnessed it will ever forget."

For if the Montagne de Bligny had gone, the French position on the Montagne de Rheims, south-west of Rheims, and the Cathedral city itself would have been endangered, no less than by the attack on the north-east of the town, which General Gouraud a month later pinned to earth. And when we reached Dormans, on the south bank, turning west-ward to Chateau Thierry, we were on ground no less vital, where in July the American troops in General Pershing's words wrote "one of the most brilliant pages in our military annals." The story is well known. The Germans were attempting to cross the river in force between Donnans and Chateau Thierry, and then to thrust their way down the valley of the Surmelin to Montmirail and the great main road to Paris, which passes through that town. A single regiment of the 3rd American Division held up the enemy, on the river bank to the east of Mezy, fighting at the same time east and west against German parties who had managed to get a footing at other points on the south side, and finally counter-attacking, throwing two German divisions into complete confusion, and capturing six hundred prisoners. No episode in the war is more likely to ring in the memory of after-times. "In the bend of the Marne at the mouth of the Surmelin," says Colonel Palmer, "not a German was able to land. In all twenty boats full of the enemy were sunk or sent drifting harmlessly down the stream." To the east of Mezy also, four American platoons did incredible things in defence of the Paris-Nancy railway. "They were not going to yield that track alive—that was the simple fact." And their losses were appalling. In the second platoon of the four engaged, all were killed except three who were wounded, and half of the third were down before they had driven the enemy from the embankment. The American graves lie all on the south side of the line—the German on the north. "We actually took over four hundred prisoners between the railroad and the river—the 6th German Grenadier Regiment was annihilated...." And the Germans never reached the Surmelin valley, or that Montmirail road on which they had set their hearts. "The deciding factor," says Colonel Palmer, "was the unflinching courage of our men, and their aggressive spirit." And the action, small as were the numbers engaged, could not have been bettered. "It is a military classic."

Over this hard-fought ground, consecrated by the graves of men who had thus bravely—thus gaily—laid down their lives for a cause of which they had no doubt, we ran on to Chateau Thierry, and that western flank of the Marne salient, where in June, while the Germans were still pressing south, and in July when Foch turned upon his trapped foe, the Americans, most of whom were for the first time in real battle, bore themselves to the astonishment and admiration of all the watching Allies. In June especially, when matters were at their worst. The capture of Bouresches, and Belleau Wood, the capture of Vaux on July 1st, the gallant help which an American machine-gun battalion gave the French in covering the French retreat across the bridge at Chateau Thierry, before it was blown up, and foiling the German attempts to cross, and the German move towards Paris, were perhaps, writes a British military authority, "the most splendid service, from a military standpoint, the Americans rendered to the Allied Cause. It was certainly the first occasion on which they really made themselves felt, and brought home to the Germans the quality of the opposition they were likely to encounter from the American Armies."

As we approached Chateau Thierry, the fog had cleared away and the night was not dark. On our railway journey to Metz a week earlier, we had seen the picturesque old place, with Hill 204 behind it, and the ruins of Vaux to the north-west, in daylight, from the south bank of the river. Now daylight had gone, but as we neared the Marne, the high ground on the curving north bank, with its scattered lights and their twinkling reflections in the water, made still a dimly beautiful setting for the much injured but still living and busy town. We crossed the temporary bridge into the crowded streets, and then as we had come a long way, we were glad to dip for tea and a twenty minutes' break into an inn crowded with Americans. Handsome, friendly fellows! I wished devoutly that it were not so late, and Paris not so far away, that I might have spent a long evening in their company. But we were all too soon on the road again for Meaux and Paris, passing slowly through the ruined streets of Vaux, with Bouresches and Belleau Wood to our right, and behind us the great main road from Soissons to Chateau Thierry, for the command of which in its northern sector, the American divisions under General Mangin, and in its southern portion those commanded by General Degoutte, had fought so stoutly last July. Altogether seven American divisions, or close upon 200,000 men, were concerned in Foch's counter-attack, which began on July 18th; and as General Pershing notes with just pride: "The place of honour in the thrust towards Soissons on the 18th was given to our 1st and 2nd divisions, in company with chosen French divisions. These two divisions captured 7,000 prisoners and over 100 guns."

What one may call the "state entry" of America into the war had thus been made, and Germany had been given full warning of what this new element in the struggle must ultimately mean, were it given time to develop. And during all these weeks of June and July, British and American ships, carrying American soldiers, came in a never-ending succession across the Atlantic. An American Army of 5,000,000 men was in contemplation, and, "Why," said the President at Baltimore in April, "limit it to 5,000,000?" While every day the British Navy kept its grim hold on the internal life of Germany, and every day was bringing the refreshed and reorganised British Army, now at the height of its striking power, nearer to the opening on August 8th of that mighty and continuous advance which ended the war.

CHAPTER VIII

"FEATURES OF THE WAR"

April 15th.

In these April days Sir Douglas Haig's latest Despatch, dated the 21st March, 1919—the first anniversary of those black days of last year!—has just been published in all the leading English newspapers. It is divided into three parts: "The Advance into Germany," "Features of the War," and "My Thanks to Commanders and Staffs." It is on the second part in particular that public attention has eagerly fastened. Nothing could well be more interesting or more important. For it contains the considered judgment of the British Commander-in-Chief on the war as a whole, so far, at least, as Great Britain is concerned. The strong and reticent man who is responsible for it broke through the limitations of official expression on two occasions only during the war: in the spring of 1917, in that famous and much criticised interview which he gave to certain French journalists, an incident, by the way, on which this Despatch throws a good deal of light; and in the impassioned Order of last April, when, like Joffre on the Marne, he told his country: that England had her back to the wall.

But here, for the first time, the mind on which for three and a half years depended the military fortunes, and therewith the future destiny of the British Empire, reveals itself with much fullness and freedom, so far as the moment permits. The student of the war cannot read these paragraphs too closely, and we may be sure that every paragraph in them will be a text for comment and illustration in the history schools of the future. The Despatch, moreover, is full of new information on points of detail, and gives figures and statistics which have never yet been made public. There are not, however, many persons outside the Armies who will give themselves to the close study of a long military despatch. Let me try, then, before I wind up these letters of mine, to bring out very shortly both some of the fresh points of view and the new detail which make the Despatch so interesting. It will be seen, I think, that the general account given in my preceding letters of British conclusions on the war, when tested by the Despatch, may still hold its own.

In the first place, the Field Marshal dwells in words of which the subdued bitterness is unmistakable, on Great Britain's unpreparedness for the war. "We were deficient in both trained men and military material, and, what is more important, had no machinery ready by which either men or material could be produced in anything like the necessary quantities." It took us, therefore, "two and a half years to reach the high-water mark of our infantry strength," and by that time we had lost thousands of lives, which, had we been better prepared, need never have been lost.

And, moreover, our unpreparedness, and the fact that we were not able to take a full share in the war till the summer of 1916, terribly wasted the man-power of France. "The excessive burden," says Marshal Haig, "thrown upon the gallant Army of France during that period caused them losses the effect of which has been felt all through the war and directly influenced its length." Meanwhile, what might have been "the effect of British intervention on a larger scale, in the earlier stages of the war, is shown by what was actually achieved by our original Expeditionary Force."

Who was responsible for this unpreparedness?

Mrs. Humphry Ward

Sir Douglas Haig does not raise the question. But those of us who remember the political history of the years from 1906 to 1914 can hardly be in doubt as to the answer. It was the Radical and anti-militarist group of the Liberal party then in power, who every year fought the Naval and Military Estimates—especially the latter—point by point, and stubbornly hampered the most necessary military provision, on whom, little as they intended or foresaw it, a tragic responsibility for the prolongation of the war, and the prodigal loss of life it involved, must always rest. Lord Haldane, indeed during his years of office as the War Minister of the Liberal Government, made a gallant fight for the Army. To him we owe the Expeditionary Force, the Territorials, the organisation of the General Staff, the Officers' Training Corps; and without his reforms our case would have been black indeed when the storm broke. No one has repelled more indignantly the common Tory charges against Lord Haldane than Sir Douglas Haig himself. But, during his years at the War Office Lord Haldane was fighting against heavy odds, attacked on the one hand by the upholders of Lord Roberts's scheme, in which neither he nor the General Staff believed, and under perpetual sniping on the other from the extreme section of his own party. The marvel is that he was able to do what he did!

Granting, however, the unpreparedness of England, what a wonderful story it is on which Sir Douglas Haig looks back! First, the necessary opening stage of this or any war—*i.e.*, a preliminary phase of manoeuvring for position, on both sides, which came to an end with "the formation of continuous trench lines from the North Sea to the Swiss frontier." Then, when British military power had developed, followed "the period of real struggle," in which the main forces of the two belligerent Armies were pitted against each other in close and costly combat—*i.e.*, "the wearing-down battle" which must go on in this war, as in all wars where large and equal forces are engaged, till one or the other combatant begins to weaken. And, finally, the last stage, when the weakening combatant stakes "on a supreme effort what reserves remain to him," and must abide by the issue. Germany staked her last reserves in the "great sortie" of her beleaguered Armies, which lasted from April to July of 1918. She lost the game, and the end, which was inevitable, followed quickly.

For the British Commander-in-Chief insists that we must look upon the war as a whole. In the earlier part of the wearing-down battle which occupied its central years, we did what we could till our new armies were ready, and without us France could not have held out. Without the British Navy, in particular, the war must have collapsed in a month. But the main brunt of the struggle on land had to be borne—and was superbly borne—by France up to the summer of 1916, when we entered on our full strength. Thenceforward the chief strain lay on the constantly developing Armies of Great Britain. From July, 1916, to the Armistice, Sir Douglas Haig bids us conceive the long succession of battles fought by the Allies in France as "one great and continuous engagement." "Violent crises of fighting" within such a conflict may appear individually as "indecisive battles." But the issue is all the time being slowly and inexorably decided. And as soon as the climax is reached, and the weakening of one side or the other begins, nothing but the entry of some new and unexpected factor can avert the inevitable end. When Russia broke down in 1917, it looked for a time as though such a new factor had appeared. It prolonged the war, and gave Germany a fresh lease of fighting strength, but it was not sufficient to secure victory. She did her utmost with it in 1918, and when she failed, the older factors that had been at work, through all the deadly progress of the preceding years of the war, were seen at last for the avengers, irresistible and final, that they truly were. "The end of the war," says the Commander-in-Chief, "was neither sudden, nor should it have been unexpected." The rapid collapse of Germany's military powers in the latter half of 1918 was the logical outcome of the fighting of the previous two years. *Attrition* and *blockade* are the two words that explain the final victory. As to the cost of that victory, the incredible heart-rending cost, Sir Douglas Haig maintains that, given the vast range of the struggle, and the vital issues on which it turned— given also the unpreparedness of England, and the breakdown of Russia, the casualties of the war could not have been less. The British casualties in all theatres of war are given as 3,000,000—2,500,000 on the Western front; the French at 4,800,000; the Italians, including killed and wounded only, 1,400,000; a total of *nine million, two hundred thousand.* On the enemy side, the Field Marshal gives the German and Austro-Hungarian losses at approximately eleven millions. And to these have to be added the Russian casualties before 1917, a figure running into millions; the Serbian, Roumanian, and Turkish losses, and, lastly, the American.

Some *seven million young men* at least have perished from this pleasant earth, which is now again renewing its spring life in beauty and joy, and millions of others will bear the physical marks of the struggle to their graves. Is there anything to console us for such a spectacle? The reply of the British Commander-in-Chief is that "the issues involved in this stupendous struggle were far greater than those concerned in any other war in recent history. Our existence as an Empire, and civilisation itself as it is understood by the free Western nations was at stake. Men fought as they had never fought before."

"Go, stranger, and tell the Lacedaemonians that we lie here, obedient to their will." So the Greek epitaph that all men know. In the same spirit, for country and home, for freedom and honour—at the Will of that Power by whom "the most ancient heavens are fresh and strong"—these fighters of our day laid down their ardent and obedient lives. There is but one way in which we can truly honour them. A better world, as their eternal memorial:—shame on us if we cannot build it!

May 20th.

Since the preceding paragraphs were written, the French General Staff has published an illuminating analysis of those military conditions in the concluding months of the war which compelled the German Command and the German

Government to sue for an Armistice. The German proclamation, when the conclusion of the Armistice allowed those
armies to retreat, proclaimed them "unconquered." Our own
Commander-in-Chief declares, it will be remembered, on the
other hand, that the fighting along the front of the British
Armies from November 1st to November 11th had "forced on
the enemy a disorderly retreat. Thereafter he was neither
capable of accepting nor refusing battle. The utter confusion of
his troops, the state of his railways, congested with abandoned
trains, the capture of huge quantities of rolling-stock and
material—all showed that our attack had been decisive.... The
strategic plan of the Allies had been realised with a
completeness rarely seen in war. When the Armistice was
signed, his defensive powers had already been definitely
destroyed. A continuance of hostilities could only have meant
disaster to the German Armies, and the armed invasion of
Germany."

To this statement from the leader of those armies to whom it
fell to strike the last decisive blows in the struggle may now be
added the testimony of the admirably served Intelligence
Department of the French General Staff, as to the precise
condition of the German Armies before the Armistice. "The
strategic plan of the Allies," of which Sir Douglas Haig speaks,
was the supreme business of Marshal Foch, and the facts and
figures now given show how closely the great Frenchman was
informed and how "completely," to use Marshal Haig's word,
his plans were carried out. On the 3rd of October Hindenburg
had written to Prince Max of Baden, that "as a result ... of our
complete inability to fill up the gaps caused by the very heavy
losses inflicted on us during the recent battles, no hope is
left ... of forcing the enemy to make peace." How true this was
is made plain by the details just published. On September
25th—that is to say, the day before the British attack on the
Hindenburg line, and the French and American attacks east
and west of the Argonne—the Intelligence Department of the
French General Staff reported to Marshal Foch that since July
15th, in the Marne salient, at St. Mihiel, and in the British
battles of Amiens, Bapaume, and the Scarpe, the enemy had

engaged 163 divisions. His reserves were reduced to 68 divisions—as against 81 in July—and of these only 21 were fresh troops. The German line had been shortened by 125 miles, but so weakened were the German Armies, that the same number of divisions had to be kept in the line as before the shortening—each division representing only some three-quarters of its former strength, and 16 divisions having been broken up to fill the ranks in those that remained.

Following immediately on this report came the three converging attacks of the Allies. On October 9th the German Army, under British pressure, abandoned the whole Hindenburg position, and entered upon a general retreat from the North Sea to the Meuse. At that moment 44 of the German divisions in line were not to be depended on for further serious fighting, and there were only 22 divisions available to replace them, of which 15 were of inferior quality, holding "quiet" sectors. On October 11th the French Intelligence Bureau reported that "it is impossible for the enemy, with the forces that he has at present in line, to stop and face any considerable attack for an appreciable time."

On October 4th, the day after Hindenburg's letter to Prince Max, the German Chancellor cabled to President Wilson, asking for an Armistice. *Already, on September 28th*, in the very midst of the British attack on the Hindenburg line, and on the morrow of General Gouraud's and General Pershing's first advances in Champagne and the Argonne, the German Command had warned the Chancellor that this step must be taken, and from October 9th onward there was no more heart left in the German Armies. The "prisoners" line in the chart,[10] brought daily up to date at the Headquarters of the British Army, shows what the demoralisation had become in the German ranks. After the British battle of the Sambre (November 4th) there were practically no reserves left, and Marshal Foch had plans in store which, had there been any further resistance, must have led to the wholesale capitulation of all that was left of the German Armies.

[10] See reproduction.

* * * * *

So in ignominy and shame the German onslaught on the liberties of Europe came—militarily—to its bitter end. The long-drawn agony of four and a half years was over, and the "wearing-out battle" had done its work. Now, six months later, we are in the midst of that stern Epilogue—in which a leagued Europe and America are dictating to Germany the penalties by which alone she may purge her desperate offence. A glance at the conditions of Peace published to the world on May 11th, the anniversary of the-sinking of the *Lusitania*, will form the natural conclusion to this imperfect survey of the last and most glorious stage in "England's Effort." But for the moment, let me return to the "Features of the War," and Marshal Haig's comments on them in his last Despatch. Many, many books will be written about them in the future! All I can do here is to single out a few of those that seem to be most commonly in the minds of those who are still thinking about the war.

* * * * *

Take, first, the value of cavalry in modern battle. In his April Despatch, Sir Douglas Haig enters on a strong defence of it— the plea of a great cavalry leader. Since the stabilisation of the trench system in the West, it has been, as we can all remember, a commonplace of the newspapers and of private conversation that cavalry were played out—a mere useless or ornamental excrescence on armies that, by the help of tanks and aeroplanes, could now excellently do without them. "Not at all," replies Sir Douglas Haig. If the German Command had had at their disposal last March and April "even two or three well-trained cavalry divisions, a wedge might have been driven between the French and British armies." In any case, the difficulties of our task would have been greatly increased. On the other hand, our cavalry were enormously useful to us in the same battle. "So great indeed became the need for mounted men that certain units which had been dismounted were hurriedly provided with horses and did splendid service. Frequently when it was impossible to move forward other troops in time our mounted troops were able to fill gaps in our line and restore the situation." During the long trench battle of the middle years "the absence of room for manoeuvre made the importance of cavalry less apparent." But in the last stage of the struggle, when the Germans "were falling back in disorganised masses," the moral effect of British cavalry pressing on the heels of the enemy was "overwhelming," and had not the Armistice stopped the cavalry advance, it would have turned the enemy's disorganised retreat "into a rout."

This is strong testimony, and will probably be stoutly fought by the eager advocates of "mechanical contrivances." But Sir Douglas Haig stands to it that no form of mechanical contrivance can ever either make the cavalryman useless, or the infantryman, who is "the backbone of defence and the spear-head of attack," less important. He admits, indeed, fully that machine guns, tanks, aeroplanes, and motor transport "have given a greater driving power to war," and that the country which possesses most of such things has an advantage over its opponents. But he insists that their only "real function" is to assist the infantry to get to grips with their opponents, and that of themselves "they cannot possibly obtain a decision." To imagine that tanks and aeroplanes can ever take the place of infantry and cavalry is to do these marvellous tools themselves a disservice by expecting of them more than they can perform. "Only by the rifle and bayonet of the infantry can the decisive victory be won." For, as the Commander-in-Chief lays down no less strongly than this great French colleague, Marshal Foch, "this war has given no new principles." But it has greatly complicated the application of the old. Every new invention makes the problem of co-operation—of interaction between the different armies and services—more difficult and more imperative.

* * * * *

As to the artillery history of the war, the Field Marshal gives the most amazing figures. When in 1916, at the suggestion of Mr. Roosevelt, and by the wish of our Government, I went through some of our leading munition districts, with a view to reporting what was being done in them to England's friends in America, the great development which started from the Munitions Act of 1915 was still only in its earlier stages. Everywhere the Government factories were rising with what seemed incredible rapidity, and the older works were doubling and trebling their output. But the output was still far behind the need. By the date of the Somme Battle, indeed—in the autumn, that is, of the same year—it had risen enormously. I may quote my own words in *England's Effort* (October, 1916): "The total amount of heavy guns and ammunition manufactured in Great Britain in the first ten months of the war would not have kept the British bombardment on the Somme *going for a single day.*"

And now?

On that first day of the Somme Battle, July, 1916, says the Despatch, "13,000 tons of ammunition were fired by us on the Western front. On the *31st of July*, 1917, in the Third Battle of Ypres, *the British Armies used* 23,000 *tons of ammunition.*" *Last year*, from August to November, 700,000 *tons of ammunition* were expended by the British Armies on the Western front. On the days of most active fighting 20,000 *tons a day* was a common ration. The supply never failed. In the three months' offensive of last autumn all the Army Commanders had to think of in the matter of artillery and ammunition was transport and distribution. The amount was unlimited. While in the matter of guns, the British Army, which on August 4th, 1914, possessed 486 pieces of different calibres, all told, at the tune of the Armistice was employing 6,437 guns and howitzers of all kinds, including the heaviest monsters of the battle-field.

And with this vast increase in material had gone perpetual advance in organisation. Artillery commanders were introduced into all armies and corps, with staffs acting under them.

Hence a greater concentration of brain and energy on the special artillery problems—very soon justified by results. Science and experience had full play, and the continuous artillery battle begun on the Somme ended, as it deserved to end, "in the defeat of the enemy's guns." To that defeat new inventions—or the marvellous development of old ones—were perpetually tending. Take sound-ranging for instance, which, with flash-spotting and air photography, has enabled the gunner more and more certainly to locate his enemy's gun while concealing the position of his own. For "the object of a gun or howitzer is to throw a projectile to some spot the position of which is *known*." The older way of knowing was by registration—throwing round after round, and by the help of aeroplane or other observation of the results, getting nearer and nearer to the target till the range was exactly found. By this method, not only is the enemy warned, but your own position is revealed. The newer method aims at *surprise*—the supreme aim of modern war.

"The principle of the location of guns by sound," writes an artillery officer, "is simple enough. Suppose there are two observers in the British lines, one at each end of a long line. Bisect this base, and from the middle point draw a line at right angles to the base and towards the German lines. Now, if a hostile gun fires from a position on this line, the sound will reach both observers simultaneously. If the gun fires from a position to the right of the line, the sound will reach the right-hand observer first, and vice versa. Then, by measuring exactly the time-interval between the arrival of the sound at each observation post, the bearing to the gun can be calculated."

"Until quite recently the Germans used four human observers, who timed the sound intervals with stop watches. The British used six microphones of a special type, connected electrically with a photographic-recording apparatus. Instead of stop watches, therefore, we used a timing device capable of recording the most minute time-intervals with perfect precision. The whole system was immeasurably superior to the German, and at least twenty times as accurate, for the British system was absolutely automatic. It recorded the arrival of the sound at the various microphones instantaneously on a permanent record; while the German system, apart from its crude method of measuring time, was subject to the combined errors of four human 'microphones.' The British system requires only one forward observer, placed well ahead of the base, and all he has to do is to press a button and start the apparatus before the sound reaches the microphones.

"The photographic record is ready for the computer in from six to ten seconds, and the gun position can be found and plotted in three or four minutes.

"Sound ranging also can be used for ranging our own guns with great accuracy. When a record has been obtained of a hostile gun, all that need be done is to record the burst of our own shell and give corrections to our battery until the record of our shell-burst is identical with that of the hostile gun. The shell must then be on the target.

"The system works equally well by day or by night, in rain or in fog. Its one enemy is a wind which blows towards the hostile gun and prevents the sound reaching the recording apparatus. It can detect a gun as easily if it is in a wood or in a building as if it were on a hill-top.

"Simple as it appears, however, it is not so easy as one might think to make a practical ally of sound ranging. We have succeeded. The Germans failed. Towards the end of the war at least ninety per cent, of the German artillery was marked down accurately by these means; and the staff employed on sound-ranging and flash-spotting (the last a kindred method depending on a mixture of observation and mathematics) had grown from *four* in 1914 *to four thousand five hundred* in 1918.

"Casualties have been heavy, and the work arduous. But those responsible for it have, at any rate, 'done their bit.'"

This is just one instance, such as we ignorant at home can

more or less follow, of that concentration of British wit and British perseverance on the terrible business of war which carried us to our goal. Germany prided herself, above all, on "scientific war." But the nation she despised as slow-witted and effete has met her again and again on her own boasted ground, and, brain for brain, has won.

With the ever-growing importance of artillery has gone, of course, a constant increase in artillery *personnel*, and in the proportion of gunners to infantry. The Third Battle of Ypres in the autumn of 1917 was "one of intense struggle for artillery supremacy," says the Field Marshal. Germany had put out all her strength in guns, and was determined to beat down the British artillery. The British Command met the attack and defeated it, in a long-drawn battle, in which, naturally, the proportion of artillery *personnel* to infantry was exceptionally high—at one time eighty-five per cent. Last spring, for a short time, owing to the transference of batteries from the Russian front, the enemy command succeeded in establishing "a definite local artillery superiority." But it was soon over. Before the breakdown of the March offensive "our guns had regained the upper hand," and in the later battles of the year the German artillery was finally mastered.

But immense as was the growth of the artillery factor, the ultimate problem was the old problem of co-operation and combination of *all factors*. "Deep study of work other than one's own," "understanding of the other man's job"—for the highest success in any branch of the Army, these were and are indispensable. Only so can the vast machine work satisfactorily; only so can the human intelligence embodied in it come to its own.

To the two subsidiary services most in the public eye—tanks and aeroplanes—I will return presently. As to the Signal Service, the "nervous system" of the Army, on which "co-operation and combination" depend, it has grown, says the Field Marshal, "almost out of recognition." At the outbreak of war it consisted of 2,400 officers and men; by the end of the war it had risen to 42,000. Cables, telegrams, wireless, carrier-pigeons and dog messengers—every kind of device was used for keeping up the communications, which mean everything in battle. The signal officer and his men creeping out over No Man's Land to mend a wire, or lay down a new one, in the very heart of the fighting, have carried the lives of thousands in their hands, and have risked their own without a thought. Sir Douglas Haig, from his Headquarters, spoke not only to every unit in the British Army, but to the Headquarters of our Allies—to London, Paris, and Marseilles. An Army Headquarters was prepared to deal with 10,000 telegrams and 5,000 letters in twenty-four hours; and wherever an army went, its cables and telephones went with it. As many as 6,500 miles of field cable have been issued in a single week, and the weekly average over the whole of 1918 was 3,000.

As to the Rearward and Transport Services, seeing that the Army was really the nation, with the best of British intelligence everywhere at its command, it is not surprising perhaps that a business people, under the pressure of a vital struggle, obtained so brilliant a success. In 1916, I saw something of the great business departments of the Army—the Army Service, Army Ordnance, and Motor Transport depots at Havre and Rouen. The sight was to me a bewildering illustration of what English "muddling" could do when put to the test. On my return to London, Dr. Page, the late American Ambassador, who during the years when America was still neutral had managed, notwithstanding, to win all our hearts, gave me an account of the experience of certain American officers in the same British bases, and the impression made on them. "They came here afterwards on their way home," he said—I well remember his phrase, "with the eyes starting out of their heads, and with reports that will transform all our similar work at home." So that we may perhaps trace some at least of those large and admirable conceptions of Base needs and Base management, with which the American Army prepared its way in France, to these early American visits and reports, as well as to the native American genius for organisation and the generosity of American finance.

But if the spectacle of "the back of the Army" was a wonderful one in 1916, it became doubly wonderful before the end of the war. The feeding strength of our forces in France rose to a total approaching 2,700,000 men. The Commander-in-Chief tries to make the British public understand something of what this figure means. Transport and shipping were, of course, the foundation of everything. While the British Fleet kept the seas and fought the submarine, the Directorate of Docks handled the ports, and the Directorate of Roads, with the Directorates of Railway Traffic, Construction and Light Railways, dealt with the land transport. During the years of war we landed ten and a half millions of persons in France, and last year the weekly tonnage arriving at French ports exceeded 175,000 tons. Meanwhile four thousand five hundred miles of road were made or kept up by the Directorate of Roads. Only they who have seen with their own eyes—or felt in their own bones!—what a wrecked road, or a road worn to pieces by motor lorries, is really like, can appreciate what this means. And during 1918 alone, the Directorate of Railway Traffic built or repaired 2,340 miles of broad-gauge and 1,348 miles of narrow-gauge railway. Everywhere, indeed, on the deserted battle-fields you come across these deserted light railways by which men and guns were fed. May one not hope that they may still be of use in the reconstruction of French towns and the revival of French agriculture?

As to the feeding and cooking and washing of the armies, the story is no less wonderful, and I remember as I read the great camp laundry at Etaples that I went through in 1917, with its busy throng of Frenchwomen at work and its 30,000 items a day. Twenty-five thousand cooks have been trained in the cookery schools of the Army, while a jealous watch has been kept on all waste and by-products under an Inspectorate of Economies. As to the care of the horses, in health or in sickness, the British Remount and Veterinary Service has been famed throughout Europe for efficiency and humanity.

Of the vast hospital service, what can one say that has not been said a thousand tunes already? Between the spring of 1916, when I first saw the fighting front, and November, 1918, the hospital accommodation in France rose from 44,000 to 175,000 persons. That is to say, we kept our wounded in France during the height of the submarine campaign, both to protect them from the chance of further suffering, and to economise our dwindling tonnage, and fresh hospitals had to be built for them. Of the doctors and nurses, the stretcher-bearers and orderlies, whose brave and sacred work it was to gather the wounded from the battle-line, and to bring to bear upon the suffering and martyrdom of war all that human skill and human tenderness could devise, Sir Douglas Haig has said many true and eloquent things in the course of his despatches. He sums them all up in his last despatch in the plain words: "In spite of the numbers dealt with, *there has been no war in which the resources of science have been utilised so generously and successfully for the quick evacuation and careful tending of the sick and wounded, or for the prevention of disease.*"

Most true—and yet? Do not let us deceive ourselves! The utmost energy, the tenderest devotion, the noblest skill, can go but a certain way when measured against the sum total of human suffering caused by war. The ablest of doctors and nurses are the first to admit it. Those of us whose wounded brothers and sons reached in safety the haven of hospital comfort and skilled nursing, and were thereby brought back to life, are, thank Heaven, the fortunate many. But there are the few for whose dear ones all that wonderful hospital and nursing science was of no avail. I think of a gallant boy lying out all night with a broken thigh in a shell-hole amid the mud and under the rain of Flanders. Kind hands come with the morning and carry him to the advanced dressing station. There is still hope. But miles of mud and broken ground lie between him and the nearest hospital. Immediate warmth and rest and nursing might have saved him. But they are unattainable. Brave men carry the boy tenderly, carefully, the three miles to the casualty clearing station. The strain on the flickering life is just too much, and in the first night of hospital, when every care is round it, the young life slips away—lost by so little—by no fault!

Is there any consolation? One only—the boy's own spirit. A comrade remembers one of his last sayings—a simple casual word: "I don't expect to come through—but—it's worth it."

There one reaches the bed-rock of it all—the conviction of a just cause. What would it avail us—this pride of victory, of organisation, of science, to which these great despatches of our great Commander-in-Chief bear witness, without that spiritual certainty behind it all—the firm faith that England was fighting for the right, and, God helping her, "could do no other."

CHAPTER IX

TANKS AND AEROPLANES

THE STAFF WORK OF THE WAR

I have quoted in the preceding chapter the warning words of Sir Douglas Haig on the subject of "mechanical appliances." The gist of them is that mechanical appliances can never replace men, and that the history of tanks in the war shows that, useful as they have been, their value depends always upon combination with both infantry and artillery. So far from their doing away with artillery, the Commander-in-Chief points out that the Battle of Amiens, August 8th, in which the greatest force of tanks was used, and in which they were most brilliantly successful, was "an action in which more artillery ammunition was expended than in any action of similar dimensions in the whole war."

The tank enthusiasts will clearly not be quite satisfied with so measured a judgment! They point to the marked effect of the tanks on the strategy of the last three months of the war, to the extraordinary increase in the elements of mobility and surprise which their use made possible, to the effect of them also on German opinion and *morale*, and they believe that in any future war—if war there be!—they are certain to play, not a subsidiary, but a commanding part.

One of the most distinguished officers of the Tank Corps, who was wounded and decorated before he joined the corps, was severely wounded twice while he belonged to the corps, and was an eye-witness of the incidents he describes, allows me to print the following letter:

"You ask me for a short account of what tanks have done in the war. In doing so, you set me a difficult problem! For three years I have thought of practically nothing else but tanks, so that I find it very difficult to deal with the subject briefly. However, I will try.

"The basic idea and purpose of tanks is a very simple one: to save infantry casualties. A new tank can be built in a few months; a new soldier cannot be produced under eighteen years. This idea—of the use of mechanical means to save casualties—undoubtedly had much to do with the production in the Tank Corps, a new unit and without traditions, of the very high *esprit de corps* it has always shown, and without which it could not have developed successfully.

"Tanks were first used by the British on the 15th September, 1916, in the Battle of the Ancre. They had, however, been designed to meet the conditions which existed *in the preceding year*, before the tremendous artillery bombardments of the middle stages of the war reduced the ground to a series of shell-holes and craters, which were so closely continuous over a large area of ground that they could not possibly be avoided. Compared with the latest type of tank, our first effort—known as Mark I.—may appear crude; but much genius had been expended upon it, and it is worth noting that both the French and German tanks, produced long after this tank, were much inferior to it.

"The Ypres salient, let me begin by saying, was never favourable to the employment of tanks. In the Third Battle of Ypres (31st July to November, 1917), which I personally believe to have been the hardest battle of the whole war, the tanks were unable to cope with the wet and shelled ground."

Nevertheless, towards the end of the Ypres battle the tank attack in the first Battle of Cambrai was being planned, and there, at last, the enthusiasts of the Tank Corps had the conditions for which they had been long hoping—a good ground and a surprise attack.

"It is important to remember, the letter continues, that the Hindenburg line at that time presented an insoluble problem. The *sea of wire* which protected its well-developed trenches and machine-gun positions was placed almost throughout on the *reverse slope* of the hills or rising ground of which the line took advantage. The artillery observer could hardly get a view of the wire at all; beside which, it was so deep it would have taken a month to cut it by artillery fire.

"*The tank provided the solution*—the only solution. The tank, by *crushing down the wire*—in a few minutes—was able to do what there seemed no other way of doing. And the tank success at Cambrai was not a mere flash in the pan. To the end of the war the Hindenburg line, or any other line organised in the same way, was entirely at the mercy of the tanks.

"The tanks, however, did not make their full weight felt until August, 1918. They had become a very important factor before that, and had saved thousands of lives; but from the beginning of the counter-offensive of last year they were a dominating feature of the war. Ludendorff had already recognised their importance in July, after the French use of them in the Battle of Soissons, when he wrote to his Army Commanders that 'the utmost attention must be paid to combating tanks. Our earlier successes against tanks led to a certain contempt for this weapon of warfare. We must now reckon with more dangerous tanks.'"

The "earlier successes" mentioned were those of the Third

Battle of Ypres. In the Ypres salient, however, the real anti-tank defence was the mud, and the general conclusions which the German Higher Command drew from the derelict tanks they captured during the fighting of October, 1917, were entirely misleading, as they soon discovered to their cost, a few weeks later, in the First Battle of Cambrai. They showed, indeed, throughout a curious lack of intelligence and foresight with regard to the new weapon, both as to its possibilities and as to the means of fighting it. They were at first entirely surprised by their appearance in the field; then they despised them; and it was not till July and August, 1918, at the beginning of the last great Allied offensive—when it will be remembered that Sir Henry Rawlinson had 400 tanks under his command—that the Germans awoke—too late—to the full importance of the new arm.

Thenceforward "the enemy was overcome by a great fear of the Allied tanks, and in some cases even over-estimated their effect." But it was now too late to put up an adequate defence against "the more dangerous tanks," which were already available in large numbers on the Allied side. It seems incredible, but it is true, that *the Germans never possessed at any time more than fifteen tanks of their own*, plus some twenty-five captured and repaired British tanks; and the only action in which they employed them with any considerable success was at the capture of Villers Bretonneux, April 24th, 1918 (the success which was so quickly turned into defeat by the Australians). After last July, however, the German panic with regard to them grew rapidly, and on the 15th of August we find it stated that everything possible must be done to give the artillery "freedom of action *in its main role*, viz., the engagement of tanks." "Its main role!" The phrase shows that under the pressure of the tanks, the two chief pillars and axioms of the former German defence system—"protective barrages" and "immediate counter-attack"—were giving way, in the case at least of tank attacks, with, of course, the natural result of confusion and weakness. After the Battle of Amiens (August 8th) the German Command issued an explanation of the defeat, signed by Ludendorff. Chief among the reasons given appears: "The fact that the troops were surprised by the massed attack of tanks, and lost their heads when the tanks suddenly appeared behind them, having broken through under cover of fog and smoke." The Crown Prince's group of armies reports on the same battle: "That during the present fighting large numbers of tanks broke through on narrow fronts, and, pushing straight forward, rapidly attacked battery positions and the headquarters of divisions. In many cases no defence could be made in time against the tanks, which attacked them from all sides."

And the peremptory order follows:

> "Messages concerning tanks will have priority over all other messages or calls whatsoever."

Naturally the German Army and the German public had by this time begun to ask why the German Command was not itself better equipped with tanks before the opening of the Allied offensive. The answer seems to be, first of all, that they were originally thought little of, as "a British idea." "The use of 300 British tanks at Cambrai," says a German document, "was a 'battle of material.' The German Higher Command decided from the very outset not to fight a 'battle of material.'" They preferred instead their habitual policy of "massed attack" —using thereby in the fighting line a number of inferior men, "classified as fit for garrison or labour duties," but who, if they "can carry a rifle, must fight." The German Command were, therefore, "not in a position to find the labour for the construction of new and additional material such as tanks." For the initial arrogance, however, which despised the tanks, and for the system which had prevented him from building them in time, when their importance was realised, the enemy was soon plunged in bitter but unavailing regrets. All he could do was to throw the blame of failure on the Allies' new weapon, and to issue despairing appeals to his own troops. The Allies were sometimes stated to have captured such and such a place "by the use of masses of tanks," when, as a matter of fact, very few tanks had been used. And this convenient excuse, as it

Mrs. Humphry Ward

appeared in the official *communiques*, began soon to have some strange and disastrous results. The German regimental officer began to think that as soon as tanks appeared, it was *a sufficient reason for the loss of a position*. For the German Army last year might be divided into three categories: "A small number of stout-hearted men (chiefly machine-gunners), who could be depended on to fight to the last; men who did not intend to fight, and *did* intend to put up their hands on the first occasion; and, thirdly, the 'great middle class,' who were prepared to do their duty, and had a sense of discipline, but who could not be classed as heroes.... It was they who came to consider that when tanks arrived, 'there was nothing to be done.'"

Moreover, the failure of the German Higher Command to produce tanks themselves to fight those of the Allies had a very serious effect, not only on the faith of the troops in their generals, but also on the *morale* of the public at home. German war correspondents and members of the Reichstag began to ask indignant questions, and the German War Office hurriedly defended itself in the Reichstag. As late as October 23rd General Scheuch, the German War Minister, declared: "We have been actively engaged for a long period in producing this weapon (which is recognised as important) in adequate numbers." It seems to be true that efforts were then being made, but not true that these efforts were of long standing. "Altogether 'slowness' was the keynote throughout of the German attitude towards the tank idea." He neither appreciated their true use nor the best means of fighting them; and even when we presented him with derelict tanks, as was soon the case on the Ancre in 1916, he failed to diagnose the creature accurately.

> "It is natural, I think," my correspondent continues, "that the British should pride themselves on being the introducers and leading exponents of this weapon. What the future will bring no one knows; but if war is to persist, there can be no doubt that mechanical means in general, and tanks in particular, must develop more and more. If

any civilised state is compelled to use force, it will, if really civilised, strive to sacrifice its wealth and its material as far as possible, rather than its human lives.

"As to incidents, you asked me for some recollections of those which had particularly impressed themselves upon me. It is hard to choose. The Third Battle of Ypres, to which I have referred, brought out many wonderful deeds of deliberate self-sacrifice. Take the following:

"In one case a section of three tanks were the only ones available to support an infantry attack. The ground over which they had to proceed was in a terrible state, and their chances of success were small. Their only chance of success, in fact, depended on their finding in the early dawn, and in the fog of battle, one single crossing over the marshy stream. The enemy front line was actually in front of this stream. The officer commanding the section considered that the only way of finding the route was on foot. With the knowledge that this meant certain death, he led his section of tanks through the bad ground under very heavy fire. He found the bridge safely, and was killed as he reached it. The tanks went on and succeeded in their mission, and many infantry lives were saved by this act of sacrifice."

Then take the case of the incident of General Elles at the First Battle of Cambrai. As my correspondent of the Tank Corps, who was in the battle, says: "In modern warfare the place of the General Commanding is almost invariably in the rear of his troops, in a position where communications are good, and where he can employ his reserves at the right moment. At this battle all the available Tanks (about four hundred) were being used. There were no reserves. So the General Commanding led the attack, flying the Tank Corps flag. He came safely through the attack, which undoubtedly owed some measure of its success to the inspiration which this act gave to the troops."

A quiet account!—given by a man who was certainly not very

Mrs. Humphry Ward

far away from his General in the affair. Let me supplement it a little by the story of Mr. Philip Gibbs, who seems to have seen as much as any correspondent might, of this wonderful "show" of the Tanks.

"For strange, unusual drama, far beyond the most fantastic imagination, this attack on the Hindenburg line before Cambrai has never been approached on the Western Front; and the first act began when the Tanks moved forward, before the dawn, towards the long wide belts of wire which they had to destroy before the rest could follow. These squadrons of Tanks were led into action by the General Commanding their corps, who carried his flag on their own Tank—a most gallant gentleman, full of enthusiasm for his monsters and their brave crews, and determined that this day would be theirs. They moved forward in small groups, several hundreds of them, rolled down the Germans' wire and trampled down its lines, and then crossed the deep gulf of the Hindenburg main line, pitching nose downward as they drew their long bodies over the parapets, and rearing themselves again with forward reach of body, and heaving themselves on to the German parados beyond.... The German troops, out of the gloom of the dawn, saw these grey inhuman creatures bearing down upon them, crushing down their wire, crossing their impregnable lines, firing fiercely from their flanks and sweeping the trenches with machine-gun bullets." A captured German officer thought "he had gone mad," as he watched the Tanks, while his men ran about in terror, trying to avoid the bursts of fire, and crying out in surrender. "What could we do?"

Meanwhile, our own men, English, Irish, and Scottish troops, went behind the Tanks, "laughing and cheering when they saw them get at the German wire and eat it up, and then head for the Hindenburg line, and cross it as though it were but a narrow ditch."

And yet, after this experience, the Germans still delayed to make Tanks! No doubt they argued that, after all, the Cambrai attack, in spite of the Tanks, had ended in a check for the

British, and in the loss of much of the ground which had been gained by the surprise attack of the "grey monsters." Meanwhile, the Russian front was rapidly breaking down, and in their exultant anticipation of the fresh forces they would soon be drawing from it to throw against the British Armies, the standing contempt of the German Command for "British ideas" and a "battle of material" won the day.

The German General Staff, therefore, maintained its refusal to spare labour and material to make Tanks, and the refusal must have seemed to them fully justified by the initial success of their March offensive. Tanks played practically no part in the fighting withdrawal of the British Armies in March and April, 1918. But all this time Tank development was going on; and the believers in Tanks were working away at the improvement of the types, convinced now, as ever, that their day would come. It dawned with the Australian attack at Villers-Bretonneux on April 24th, when the fortunes of battle were already changing; it rose higher on July 4th, when the Australians again took Hamel and Vaire Wood, the Tanks splendidly helping; it was at the full on and after August 8th, at the Battle of Amiens, the first page in the last chapter of the war.

The next incident described by my correspondent occurred at the taking of the St. Quentin section of the Hindenburg line by the 4th British Army, two American divisions leading the way.

"The attack," he writes, "had been a very difficult one, and had only been successful in certain sectors. As usual, the attack had been launched at dawn, and the morning had been exceptionally misty. Later on the mist began to roll away rather quickly, and it was found that in one sector where the attack had made no progress, the Germans were in a position" —owing to the ridge they occupied having been till then shrouded in mist—"to bring very heavy machine-gun fire to bear on the backs of the troops advancing in a sector where the attack had gone well. Unless something were done at once to drive the Germans from the ridge they were holding, not only would many lives be lost, but the result of the attack which had gone well would be jeopardised. Without waiting for orders and on their own initiative, two Tanks, which were standing by in order to attack with fresh troops later in the day, drove straight for the ridge.[11] *Two Tanks, without either infantry or artillery support, went straight for an unbroken portion of the German line.* They reached the ridge, and drove the Germans off it. Both Tanks were hit by several shells, and caught fire. The survivors of the crews, with a few infantry soldiers, organised the ridge for defence, turned the German machine guns round, and when the Germans counter-attacked, this small but determined garrison poured so hot a fire on them from their own guns that they were driven back, and the important post secured."

[11] The italics are mine.

There is nothing, I think, that need prevent me from pointing out, what there is no hint of in the letter itself—that the writer of it was in one of the Tanks, and was severely wounded.

In the last actions of the war, even the semblance of a Tank was sometimes enough! "Supply Tanks"—writes my informant —"were then being used, which looked like the real thing, but were only very slightly armoured. They were intended to carry material, sometimes munitions, and even food. Three of these pseudo-tanks were carrying up material to rebuild a bridge which had been destroyed. They discovered, when they neared the place, that the enemy were holding it in some strength, and our infantry could not advance. Moreover directly the Tanks appeared, they began to draw fire—which they were not meant to face—and the situation was threatening. But, with great pluck and resource, the Tanks decided just to go on, and trust to their looks, which were like those of the fighting Tanks, to drive the enemy from the position.... One Tank became a casualty; but the other two went straight for the German lines; and the Germans, under the impression that they were being attacked by fighting Tanks, either put up their hands or fled."

Thus, in its last moments of resistance, the German Army, now but the ghost of itself, was scattered by the ghost of a Tank! What was being prepared for it, had the struggle gone on, is told in a memorandum on Tanks organisation which has come my way, and makes one alternately shudder at the war that might have been, and rejoice in the peace that is. In the last weeks of the war, Tank organisation was going rapidly forward. A new Tank Board, consisting of Naval, Military, and Industrial members, was concentrating all its stored knowledge on "the application of naval tactics to land warfare," in other words, on the development of Tanks, and had the war continued, the complete destruction of the German Armies would have been brought about in 1919 by "a Tank programme of some *six thousand machines.*" When one considers that for the whole of the three last victorious months in which Tanks played such an astonishing part, the British Armies never possessed more than four hundred of them, who travelled like a circus from army to army, the significance of this figure will be understood. Nor could Germany, by any possibility, have produced either the labour or the material necessary, whereby to meet Tank with Tank. The game was played out and the stakes lost.

*   *   *   *   *

But of fresh headings in this last tremendous chapter of *England's Effort*, there might be no end. I can only glance at one or two of them.

The Air Force? Ah, that, indeed, is another story—and so great a one, that all I can attempt here is to put together[12] a few facts and figures, in one of those comparisons of the "beginning," with the "end," of time with time, by which alone some deposit from the stream of history in which we are all bathed filters into the mind, and—with good luck: stays there. Here, in Hertfordshire, in the first summer of the war, how great an event was still the passage of an aeroplane over these quiet woods! How the accidents of the first two years appalled us, heart-broken spectators, and the inexorable military comment upon them: "Accidents or no accidents, we have got to master this thing, and master the Germans in it." And, accidents or no accidents, the young men of Britain and France steadily made their way to the aviation schools, having no illusions at all, in those early days, as to the special and deadly risks to be run, yet determined to run them, partly from clear-eyed patriotism, partly from that natural call of the blood which makes an Englishman or a Frenchman delight in danger and the untried for their own sakes. Thenceforward, the wonderful tale ran, mounting to its climax. At the beginning of the war the military wing of the British Air Service consisted of 1,844 officers and men. At the conclusion of the war there were, in round numbers, 28,000 officers and 264,000 other ranks employed under the Air Board. From under 2,000 to nearly 300,000!—and in four years! And the uses to which this new Army of the Winds was put, grew perpetually with its growth. Let us remember that, while aeroplane *reconnaissance* was of immense service in the earliest actions of the war, *there was no artillery observation by aeroplane till after the first Battle of the Marne.* There is the landmark. Artillery observation was used for the first time at the Battle of the Aisne, in the German retreat from the Marne. Thenceforward, month by month, the men in the clouds became increasingly the indispensable guides and allies of the men on the ground, searching out and signalling the guns of the enemy, while preventing his fliers from searching out and signalling our own. Next came the marvellous development of aerial photography, by which the whole trench world, the artillery positions and *hinterland* of the hostile army could be mapped day by day for the information of those attacking it; the development of the bombing squadrons, which began by harassing the enemy's communications immediately behind the fighting line, and developed into those formidable expeditions of the Independent Force into Germany itself, which so largely influenced the later months of the war. Finally, the airman, not content with his own perpetual and deadly fighting in the air, fighting in which the combatants of all nations developed a daring beyond the dreams of any earlier world, began to take part in the actual land-battle itself, swooping on reserves, firing into troops on the march, or bringing up ammunition.

[12] From the recent Official Report issued by the Air Board.

And while the flying Army of the Winds was there developing, the flying Army of the Seas, its twin brother, was not a whit behind. The record of the Naval Air Service, as the scouts for the Fleet, the perpetual foe of, and ceaseless spy upon, the submarine, will stir the instincts for song and story in our race while song and story remain. It was the naval airmen who protected and made possible the safe withdrawal of the troops from Suvla and Helles; it was they who discovered and destroyed the mines along our coasts; who fought the enemy seaplanes man to man, and gun to gun; who gave the pirate nests of Zeebrugge and Ostend no rest by day or night, who watched over the ceaseless coming and going of the British, Dominion, and American troops across the Channel; who were the eyes of our coasts as the ships, laden with the men, food, and munitions, which were the life-blood of the Allied Cause, drew homeward to our ports, with the submarines on their track, and the protecting destroyers at their side.

Nor did we only manufacture planes and train men for ourselves. "The Government of the United States," says the Air Service Report, "has paid a striking tribute to the British Air Service by adopting our system of training. The first 500 American officer cadets to be trained went through the School of Military Aeronautics at Oxford, afterwards graduating at various aerodromes in England. These officers formed the nucleus of American schools, which were eventually started both in the United States and in France.... In all about 700 American pilots have passed through our schools.... And when the question of producing a standardised engine was considered every facility was given and all our experience placed at the disposal of the American Government, with the result that the Liberty engine was evolved."

Meanwhile the constant adaptation to new conditions required in the force stimulated the wits of everybody concerned. Take aerial photography. The first successful photograph was taken in November, 1914, of the village of Neuve Chapelle. The photographic section then consisted of two officers and three men, with two cameras and a portable box of chemicals. At the present day it contains 250 officers and 3,000 men—with a large training school; and its prints have been issued by the million.

Meanwhile the development of our aircraft fire had driven the aerial photographer from a height of 3,000 feet up to a height of 22,000, where, but for invention, he might have perished with cold, or found it impossible to breathe. But intelligence pursued him, providing him with oxygen and with electric heating apparatus in the upper air. And when, on the other hand, he or his comrade swooped down to within a few hundred feet of the earth, in order to co-operate in attack with infantry or Tanks, again intelligence came into play, inventing a special armoured machine for the protection of the new tactics.

The growth of "wireless," as a means of air-communication, is another astounding chapter in this incredible story. Only *one* of the machines which left with the original Expeditionary Force was fitted with "wireless" apparatus, and it was not used till the first Battle of the Aisne, when co-operation with the artillery first began. There are now 520 officers in the "wireless" branch and 6,200 other ranks; while there are 80 "wireless" stations in France alone and several hundred battery stations. "Wireless" telephony, too, has been made practical since 1917; and over a range of some 75 miles has been of deadly use to the artillery, especially at night, when the watcher in the skies becomes aware of lighted aerodromes, or railway stations, behind the enemy lines.

"Many wonders there be, but none more wonderful than man," said Sophocles, in the fifth century before Christ, and he gives the catalogue of man's discoveries, as the reflective Greek saw it, at that moment of the world's history. Man, "master of cunning," had made for himself ships, ploughs, and houses, had tamed the horse and the bull; had learned how to snare wild creatures for food, had developed speech, intelligence, civilisation. Marvels indeed! But had it ever occurred to such a Greek to ponder the general stimulus given to human faculty by war? Probably, for the wise Greek had thought of most things, and some reader of these pages who knows his rich literature better than I do, will very likely remember how and where. Modern history, indeed, is full of examples, from the Crusades onward. But there can never have been any such demonstration of it as this war has yielded. The business of peace is now, largely, to turn to account the discoveries of the war—in mechanics, chemistry, electricity, medical science, methods of organisation, and a score of other branches of human knowledge, and that in the interests of life, and not of death. For the human loss of the war there is no comfort, except in those spiritual hopes and convictions by which ultimately most men live. But for the huge economic waste, the waste of money and material and accumulated plant, caused by the struggle, there *is* some comfort, in this development of faculty, this pushing forward of human knowledge into regions hitherto unmapped, which the war has seen. This week, for instance,[13] American and British airmen are competing in the first Atlantic flight, and the whole world is looking on. Again there is risk of danger and death, but the prizes sought are now the prizes of peace, the closer brotherhood of men, a truer knowledge one of another, the interchanges of science and labour; and they are sought by means taught in the furnace of war. Thus, from the sacrifices of the terrible past may spring a quickened life for the new world. Will that new world be worthy of them?—there is the question on which all depends. A certain anguish clings to it, as one measures the loss, and cannot yet measure the gain.

[13] May 19th.

*   *   *   *   *

        Mrs. Humphry Ward

I have dwelt on some of the accomplished wonders—the *results* of the war, in the material field—guns, Tanks, and aeroplanes. But just as mechanical devices were and are, in the opinion of the Commander-in-Chief, of no avail without the fighting men who use them; so behind the whole red pageant of the war lie two omnipresent forces without which it could not have been sustained for a day—Labour at the base, Directing Intelligence at the top. In the Labour battalions of the Army there has been a growth in numbers and a development in organisation only second to that of the fighting Army itself. Labour companies were already in being in 1914, but they chiefly worked at the ports, and were recruited mainly from dock labourers. Then it was realised that to employ the trained soldier on many of the ordinary "fatigue" duties was to waste his training, and Labour began to be sent plentifully to the front. For trench-digging, for hut-building, for the making and repair of roads and railways, for the handling and unloading of supplies and ammunition, for sanitation, salvage, moving the wounded at casualty clearing stations, and a score of other needs, the demand on the Labour battalions grew and grew.

How well I remember the shivering Kaffir boys and Indians at work on the handling of stores and ammunition in the cold spring of 1917!—and the navvy battalions on the roads before the Chinese had arrived in force, and before the great rush of German prisoners began. Between the British navvy battalions, many of them elderly men past military age, or else unfit in some way for the fighting line, and their comrades in the trenches, there were generally the friendliest relations. The fighting man knew well what he owed to the "old boys." I have before me an account by a Highland officer of the relation between a navvy and a regular battalion in the Ypres salient. "Their huts stretched along the side of the road which led us towards our trenches; and every time we passed that way the sound of the pipes would bring them out of their billets in crowds to cheer us in, or to welcome us back if we were returning. They kept that road in splendid repair, despite the heavy wear and tear of the endless traffic which used it, and we blessed them many times. There was a two-miles stretch across shell-torn, muddy country just behind the fighting line. Tired men, just relieved from the trenches, and carrying heavy equipment, naturally loathed it as a Slough of Despond; but when we struck the good, honest surface of the navvy battalion's road, though there were many miles still between us and rest, we felt the journey was as good as over, so easy, by comparison, had marching become. A close friendship grew up between our battalions. Our officers invited their officers to dinner. Our men saluted their officers, and if one of our officers happened to come on the scene of their operations, some old veteran, wearing perhaps the medal ribbon of campaigns dating back a generation, would call his gang to attention, and gravely give the salute after the manner of thirty years ago. And when one realised what the age of these men must be, who were wearing decorations of Egyptian and Indian frontier campaigns, with not a few Zulu ribbons among them, one marvelled at the skill and strength with which the old fellows wielded pick and shovel. They could not march any great distance, and we helped them along in motor buses; but once set them down by their tracks, though the road might be chaos and the shell-holes innumerable, obstacles were cleared away, holes filled up, and the new surface well and truly laid with a magical rapidity.... The idea of taking shelter never seemed to occur to them; they openly rejoiced at being under fire.... Perhaps though they mended our roads and gave us easy walking, they helped us most by the quiet steadfastness of their example. One never saw them toiling away in the deathtrap of the Ypres salient without realising that they were the fathers of our generation, men who had already spent themselves in Britain's cause when we were children, and had now come out to serve her again, at her call, and to watch how we young ones played up."

Some more recent notes from G.H.Q. dwell warmly on the invaluable services rendered by the Labour Corps in the Battle of Cambrai, November, 1917, in the defensive battle of last spring, and in the autumn attacks which ended the war. In the Cambrai attack the Labour men were concentrated 1,000 yards behind the line, so as to be ready for immediate advance.

A light railway was run into Marcoing within twenty-four hours of its capture, and another into Moeuvres under heavy fire, while the approaches to the bridges over the Canal du Nord were carried out by men working only 1,000 yards from the enemy machine guns posted on one of the locks of the Canal. In the withdrawals of last March and April, throughout the heavy defensive fighting of those dangerous weeks, no men were steadier. Theirs was the heavy work of digging new defence lines—at night—with long marches to and from their billets. Casualties and wastage were heavy, but could not be helped, as fighting men could not be spared. Yet the units concerned behaved "with the greatest gallantry." "One company," says a report from G.H.Q., "worked day and night in a forward ammunition dump for three days, and then marched seventy miles in six days, working a day and night in another ammunition dump on the way, with no transport but one G.S. wagon to help them; in their retirements, effected as they were with almost no transport, they lost practically all their equipment, and yet without getting time to rest and re-equip, they had to be moved at once to work on defence lines."

The total number of Labour men employed in stemming the German rush on Amiens, by the construction of new lines of defence, was no less than 62,000—two-thirds, nearly, of the whole British Army at Waterloo!

Then, when our counter-attack began, the task of the Labour men was reversed. Now it was for them to go forward, well ahead of the reserves, and some 1,000 yards ahead of the skilled transport troops and the construction trains that were laying the line for which the Labour men prepared the way. Death or wounds were always in the day's risks, but the Labour men "held on." By this time there were 350,000 men under the Labour Directorate—a force about equal to our whole Territorial and Regular Army before the war. They were a strange and motley host!—95,000 British, 84,000 Chinese, 138,000 Prisoners of War, 1,500 Cape Coloured, 4,000 West Indians, 11,000 South African natives, 100 Fijians, 7,500 Egyptians, 1,500 Indians—so run the principal items. The catalogue given of their labours covers all the rough work of the war household. They were the handy men everywhere, adding on occasion forestry and agriculture to their war-work, and the British Labour battalions were, of course, the stiffening and superintending element for the rest.

In the handling of the Coloured Labour Units there were naturally many new and occasionally surprising things to be learnt by the British soldiers directing them. A party of Nagas, for instance, were among the Indian Labour Units. "They were savages from a country which has only recently been brought thoroughly under British rule," writes an officer of the A.G.'s department. "Their pastime is head-hunting, and their 'uniform' when at home is that bestowed on them by Nature. They were extraordinarily cheerful, willing workers, and gave no trouble at all. The trouble of providing the special kind of food which in general the natives of India require, was entirely absent in the case of the Nagas. They have a strong liking for rats, and the only food they object to is monkeys. A company of Nagas, about May, 1917, after the advance at Arras in April, were sent up to somewhere near Boisleux to bury dead horses. The dead horses were disposed of—but not by burial. And in addition an Infantry Brigade in the neighbourhood had soon to mourn the loss of all their dogs."

The Chinese were a constant source of amusement and interest to the British. All that neatness and delicacy of finger which is shown in Chinese art and hand-work, the infinite pains, the careful finish which the Chinaman inherits from his age-long, patient past, were to be seen even in the digging of trenches. Their defence lines were a marvel of finish, in spite of the fact that in hard manual labour they were ahead of any other unit—shifting, often, 240 cubic feet of soil per day, per man. As porters, too, they were beyond rivalry; and their contempt for the German prisoners' capacity in this direction was amusing. A Chinese coolie, watching two prisoners handle a stack of cased goods, could not at last contain himself. He walked up to them, saying: "Hun no damn good," and proceeded to show them how it should be done. The stolidity of the Chinaman is generally proof against surprise, but some of those coming from the backwoods of Northern China were occasionally bewildered and overwhelmed when set down amid the amazing and to them terrifying wonders of the "back" of a European Army. One company of such men arrived at their appointed camp, and the next day there was a fight with enemy aeroplanes overhead. One of the poor coolies was so terrified that he went and hanged himself, and the rest could only be pacified with great difficulty. On the other hand, a flying officer once offered a ride to a Chinese ganger who, with his men, had been doing some work on an aerodrome for the R.A.F. "The ganger went up with glee; and the pilot's feelings may be imagined when, at a good height, he looked round and saw the ganger standing up, as happy as could be, looking over the edge and pointing down to the camp where his company lived, and other landmarks he was able to recognise."

*   *   *   *   *

Of the noble army of women, who, since 1917, have formed part of that great force behind the fighting lines I have been rapidly sketching—what shall one say but good and grateful things?

In 1917, as our car wound through the narrow streets of Montreuil, I remember noticing a yellow car in front of us, unlike the usual Army car, and was told that it contained the new head of the Women's Army Auxiliary Corps, and that 10,000 women were now to be drafted into France, to take the place of men wanted for the fighting line. And a little later at Abbeville I found General Asser, then Inspector-General of the Lines of Communication, deep in the problems connected with the housing and distribution of the new Women's Contingent. "Two women want the accommodation of three men; but three women can only do the work of two men." That seemed to be the root fact of the moment, and accommodation and work were being calculated accordingly. Then the women came, and took their place in the clerical staffs of the various military departments, of Army or other Headquarters, in the Army canteens, in the warehouses and depots of the ports. It is clear that, during the concluding year of the war, they rendered services of which British women may reasonably be proud; and in the retreat of last March, by universal testimony, they bore themselves with special coolness and pluck. Many of them were suddenly involved in the rush and confusion of battle, which was never meant to come near them. They took the risks and bore the strain of it with admirable composure. The men beside whom they marched or rode when depots canteens, and headquarters disappeared in the general over-running of our fighting lines, took note! It was yet another page in that history of a new Womanhood we are all collaborating in to-day. And I will add a last touch, within my personal knowledge, when in January, at Montreuil, in a room at G.H.Q., an officer of A. described to me how he had recently interviewed a gathering of women belonging to Queen Mary's Auxiliary Army Corps, and had asked them whether they wished to be immediately demobilised. Almost without exception the answer came: "Not while we can be useful to the Army." They had enlisted for the war; the war was not over, in spite of the Armistice; and, though it would be pleasant to go home, they still stuck to their job.

*   *   *   *   *

Thus hastily I have run through the labour of various kinds which was the base and condition of the fighting force. I have left myself room for only a few last words as to that Directing Intelligence which was its brain and soul—*i.e.*, the Staff work of the Army—from the brilliant and distinguished men at General Headquarters immediately surrounding the Commander-in-Chief, down to the Brigade and Battalion Staffs, the members of which actually conduct the daily and nightly operations of war from the close neighbourhood of the fighting line. In a preceding chapter I have given a general outline of the duties falling to the Staff of the First Army in the attack on the Hindenburg line. The range and variety of them was immense. But their success, no less than the success of the campaign as a whole, depended on the faithful execution of all the minor Staff work of the Army, from the battalion upward. The skill, precision and personal bravery required from the officers concerned are not as much realised, I think, as they ought to be by the public at home. An officer engaged as a Brigade-Major in the fight on the Ancre, September, 1917, has written me a detailed account of four days' experience in that battle, involving the relief of one brigade by another, and a successful but difficult attack, which gives a vivid idea of Staff work as carried on in the actual fighting line itself. We see, first, the night journey of the four infantry battalions and their machine-gun company and trench-mortar battery, from Albert to Pozieres by motor-bus, then the four-mile march of the troops in darkness and rain along a duck-board track, to the trenches they were to relieve. The Brigade-Major describes the elaborate preparation needed for every movement of the relief and the attack, and the anxiety in the Brigade Headquarters, a dug-out twenty feet below the ground, when the telephone— which is constantly cut by shell fire—fails to announce the arrival of each company at its appointed place. Presently, the left company of the battalion on the left is missing. In the darkness, and the congestion of men moving up to and back from the trenches on the narrow track, clearly something has gone wrong. The Brigade-Major sets out to discover the why and wherefore. The attack is to start at 6 A.M., and from 9 P.M. till nearly 5 A.M.—that is, *for close on eight hours*, the Brigade-Major is up and down the track, inquiring into the causes of delay—(a trench, for instance, has been blown in at one point, and the men forced into the mud beside it)— watching and helping the assembly of the troops, and "hunting" for the company which has not arrived, and is "apparently lost." About five he returns to his brigade, hoping for the best.

Then, half an hour before the moment appointed for the advance, "we heard a bombardment starting. The enemy had either discovered the hour of our attack, or were about to attack us." The Brigadier and his Brigade-Major anxiously go up to the top of their dug-out to survey the field. It is clear that the British line is being heavily attacked. Messages begin to arrive from the battalion commander on the left to say that all communication with his companies has now been cut. The commander on the right also rings up to report heavy casualties. Then the telephone wires on both sides are broken, and the Staff signal officer goes out to repair them under fire. At last, precisely at the moment appointed, five minutes past six, in the rainy autumn dawn, our own guns—an enormous concentration of them—open a tremendous fire, and the earth-shaking noise "helps men to forget themselves, and go blind for the enemy." Then steadily the artillery barrage goes forward, one hundred yards every four minutes, and the infantry advance behind it, past the German front trench, to a ravine about three hundred yards further, which is known to be strongly held. The final objective is a strong German position protecting a village in the valley of the Ancre.

Meanwhile, in the headquarters' dug-out, messages come pouring in "by telephone, by lamp-signal, by wireless, by pigeon, by runners, and reports dropped from aeroplanes." The progress of the battle is marked on the maps spread out on a table in the dug-out, and the Brigadier has to decide when his reserve battalion must be sent forward to assist. Information is scanty and contradictory, but "at half-hourly intervals the situation, as we believed it to be, was telephoned to our Divisional Headquarters and to the brigades on either flank." Reports come in of success at certain places and a check at others; also of a German counter-attack. All reports agree that casualties have been heavy. The ravine, indeed, has been taken with seven hundred prisoners, but the situation is still so obscure that "the Brigadier sent me out to find out the real situation."

"So I started out with an orderly." The direct route to be taken was under fire and had to be circumvented. "I was making for an old dug-out in a small ravine, where some men of our left attacking battalion had suffered heavily whilst assembling prior to the attack. The area was still being shelled, and we made a bolt for the dug-out, which we reached safely." In the dug-out is the commander of the support battalion, who reports that the commanders of the attacking battalions have gone forward to the big ravine. "I found out all I could from him, and then went forward with him to the ravine." On the way the Staff officer notices that the wire entanglements in front of the German trenches are still formidable and have not been properly cut by our artillery. "When we reached the big ravine we crawled down the steep bank to the bottom of it, and the first sight that we saw was the entrance to a German dug-out, with its previous occupants lying at the mouth of it.... I then found the commander of the left attacking battalion, who had established his headquarters in an old German dug-out." From him the Brigade-Major hears a ghastly tale of casualties. Not a single officer left, with any of his four attacking companies! Yet in spite of the loss of all their company officers, and of the fact that the left company of the battalion had been practically wiped out before the attack started, the greater portion of the battalion, led by their regimental sergeant-major, had reached their final objective.... "It was certainly," says the Brigade-Major quietly, "a very magnificent performance."

Meanwhile he finds the commander of the right battalion further up the ravine. The greater portion of the support battalion is also in the ravine. Here there were elements of three battalions, considerably disorganised, suffering from want of sleep and a terribly hard time. The commanders, dead beat, want reinforcements, and take a pessimist view. The Brigade-Major, coming fresh, thinks, on the contrary, that there are already too many men on the ground, who only want reorganising. To satisfy himself he goes forward, with the adjutant of the right battalion, to find out "exactly where our leading troops were and in what condition."

"I satisfied myself of the exact situation, and having visited the troops of the brigades on both flanks, went back to the ravine, and from one of the battalion headquarters telephoned to my Brigadier and told him what I had found out. I mentioned that both the battalion commanders said they needed more troops to reinforce them, but added that in my opinion there were already sufficient troops on the spot, and that all that was necessary was that they should be placed under the command of one officer, and reorganised by battalions, to hold their present positions. I told him everything I knew, and tried to give him a good idea of the condition of the troops on the spot. He then sent orders to me that the senior battalion commander was to assume command of all troops on the brigade front, and that under his orders they were to be reorganised into battalions and companies, in order that the defence should be as strong and efficient as possible. I then returned to Brigade Headquarters to tell my Brigadier more fully what I had seen."

The following night the brigade was relieved, after what was on the whole a very successful action. All the officers responsible for its Staff work seem to have been on duty, without rest or sleep, for some thirty-six hours, and after the attack was over there were still German prisoners to be examined.

Such is Staff work in the actual battle-line. What it needs of will, courage, and endurance will be clear, I think, to anyone reading this account, and the experience may be taken as typical of thousands like it at every stage of the war, so long as it was a war of trenches and positions. And what is also typical is that while the personal risks of the writer are scarcely hinted at, his mind, amid all his cares of superintendence and organisation, is still passionately alive to the individual risks and sufferings of his comrades. He ends on what he calls "another small point which deserves mention":

"When the officers and men of those two attacking battalions lay in the mud on that pitch-black night, soaked to the skin and shivering with cold, as they lay there waiting for the awful hour when it seems as if horror itself has been let loose, and as they wondered in their own minds what lay before them, gradually the German bombardment started, and then by degrees increased in intensity, until for fully thirty minutes before zero hour it became perfect hell.

Every one of those officers and men, without a doubt, realised that the enemy had discovered that he was going to be attacked, and that he would be on the alert and waiting for them. Yet did any one of them falter, did any one of them for a single moment dream of not starting with the rest of his comrades and doing what he knew it was his duty to do?"

"I only know two things: Firstly, that a very great number of them, if not all, realised only too well that the enemy had discovered our plans; and, secondly, that the only ones who did not start were those who could not, because they had been either killed or wounded."

And now turn with me to the top of all—the General Staff of the Army in France—the brain of the whole mighty movement. It was with no light emotion that I found myself last January, on a bitter winter day, among a labyrinth of small rooms running round the quadrangle of the old Ecole Militaire at Montreuil, while they were still full of Staff officers gathering up the records of the war. Here, or in the Staff train moving with the Commander-in-Chief along the front, the vast organisation of battle culminated in a few guiding brains from which energising and unifying direction flowed out to all parts of the field of war. Here were the heads of Q., of A., of G.—in other words, of Supply, Reinforcement, and Operations. In a bare room, with a few chairs and tables and an iron stove, the Director of Operations was at work; close by was the office of the Quartermaster-General, while up another staircase and along another narrow passage were the quarters of the Adjutant-General; and somewhere, I suppose, in the now historic building, was or had been the office of the Commander-in-Chief himself. The Intelligence Department was not far off, I knew, in the old town; I had been its grateful guest in 1917. The directing Intelligence of the Army flowed out from here to the front, while from the front, at the same time, there came back a constant stream of practical knowledge and experience, keeping the life of G.H.Q. perpetually fresh, correcting theory by experience and kindling experience by theory. The complexities and responsibilities of the work done were vast indeed.

"At any time," says an officer of the General Staff, "during the operations of the past year, work was commenced here in the office, or on the train, when G.H.Q. was advanced nearer the battle-line, at any hour before nine o'clock. The work to be done consists, in general terms, of co-ordinating all the arrangements for the operations undertaken and carried out by the several armies; the issuing of general orders and instructions for operations, the details of which were worked out by the armies concerned; the issuing of orders for the movement of divisions, of artillery units, cavalry, and Tanks—in fact, all the different services which go to make up the Army. These orders must be so arranged as to fit in with the roads and railway facilities, or the mechanical transport available, and must be so couched as not to interfere or clash with arrangements made by the armies in the Army areas. This necessitates very intimate *liaison* with the armies and with the departments concerned. Maps have to be kept up to date, showing the dispositions of troops at all times, both on the battle-front and in back areas.

"In addition, there are the arrangements with our Allies, the fixing of areas between ourselves and our Allies, and between our own armies and the lines of communication. During operations messages have to be sent out giving information of the situation to the troops, to the public, and to the War Office at home. Schemes are worked out beforehand to deal with any possible eventuality, so that in the event of a hostile attack the movement of troops may be carried out with the least possible delay. Similar schemes are worked out for operations to be undertaken by ourselves, and methods of attack are thrashed out in consultation with the Army Commanders and Staff. The various details of this work fill in the day very thoroughly. This office (of Operations) rarely closes before midnight, and the principal

Mrs. Humphry Ward

officers are frequently at work until the small hours of the morning. There is, of course, an officer on duty all night.

"During the German attack in March the officer responsible here for the movement of troops by rail did not leave the office even for meals for a number of days on end."

So the long ascent climbs, from the humblest platoon in the field, through company, battalion, division, corps, and Army to the General Staff, and the British Commander-in-Chief, moving and directing the whole; with beyond these, again, as the apex of the great construction, the figure of the illustrious Frenchman, who for the last six months of the war, by the common consent of the Allies, and especially by the free will of England and her soldiers, held the general scheme of battle in his hands. In the British Army what we have been watching is an active hierarchy of duty, discipline, loyalty, intelligence—the creation of a whole people, bent on victory for a great cause. Must it, indeed, vanish with the war, like a dream at cock-crow, or shall we yet see its marvellous training, its developments of mind and character, gradually take other shapes and enter into other combinations—for the saving and not the slaying of men?

EPILOGUE

June 1st.

I have thus brought these rapid notes—partly of things seen, partly of things read—to an end. They might, of course, go on for ever, and as I write I seem to see rising before me those libraries of the future, into which will come crowding the vast throng of books dealing in ever greater and greater detail with the events of the war and the causes of victory. But this slight summary sketch of the military events, and especially of the final "effort" of England and the Empire, in the campaign of last year, which I set myself to do, is accomplished, however inadequately. Except, indeed, for one huge omission which every reader of these few pages will at once suggest. I have made only a few references here and there to the British Navy. Yet on the British Navy, as we all know, everything hung. If the Navy could not have protected our shores, and broken the submarine peril; if the British Admiralty had not been able to hold the Channel against the enemy and ward him off from the coasts and ports of France; if the British ships and British destroyers had not been there to bring over 70 per cent of the American Armies, and food both for ourselves and the Allies; if the sea-routes between us and our Colonies, between us and the East, could not have been maintained, Germany at this moment would have been ruling triumphant over a prostrate world. The existence and power of the Navy have been as vital to us as the air we breathed and the sun which kept us alive, and the pressure of the British blockade was, perhaps, the dominating element in the victory of the Allies. But these things are so great and so evident that it seemed in this little book best to take them for granted. They have been the presuppositions of all the rest. What has not yet been so clear—or so I venture to think—to our own people or our Allies, has been the full glory of the part played by the Armies of the British Empire in the concluding phases of the war. The temporary success of the German sortie of last spring—a mere episode in the great whole—made so deep an impression on the mind of this nation, that the real facts of an *annus mirabilis*, in their true order and proportion, are only now, perhaps, becoming plain to us. It was in order to help ever so little in this process that I have tried to tell, as it appears to me, the end of that marvellous story of which I sketched the beginnings in *England's Effort*.

These main facts, it seems to me, can hardly be challenged by any future pressure from that vast critical process which the next generation, and generations after, will bring to bear upon the war. The mistakes made, the blunders here, or short-comings there, of England's mighty effort, will be all canvassed and exposed soon enough. The process indeed has already begun. And when the first mood of thankful relief from the constant pre-occupation of the war is over, we may expect to see it in full blast. It would have been easy here to repeat some of the current discontents of the day, all of which will have their legitimate hearing in future discussion. But this is not the moment, nor is mine the pen. We are but just emerging from the shadow of that peril from which the British and Imperial Armies—bone of our bone and flesh or our flesh—have saved us. Let us now, if ever, praise the "famous men" of the war, and gather into our hearts the daily efforts, the countless sacrifices of countless thousands, in virtue of which we now live our quiet lives.

Nor have I dwelt much upon the terrible background of the whole scene, the physical horror, the anguish and suffering of war. Our noblest dead, to judge from the most impassioned and inspired utterances of the men who have suffered for us, would bid us indeed remember these things,—remember them with all the intensity of which we are capable—but with few words. They never counted the cost, though they knew it well; and what they set out to do, they have done.

Let us then, at this particular moment, dwell, above all, on *the thing achieved*. To that end, a few colossal figures must still be added to those already given. Since the beginning of the war, the total forces employed by the British Empire in the various theatres of war, have amounted to a total of *eight million, six hundred and fifty-four thousand* (24 per cent of the total white male population), of which the United Kingdom supplied 5,704,416 (25.36 per cent), and the Dominions, and Colonies, 1,425,864. The Indian and Coloured troops amounted to 1,524,000. If the Navy, the Merchant Service, and the men and women employed in various auxiliary military services at home are added, the total recruiting effort of the Empire reaches to much more than *ten millions*.

As to the financial part of this country in the war, by March 22nd, 1919, the war expenditure of Great Britain had reached a total of L9,482,442,482, of which rather more than *two thousand five hundred millions* have been raised by taxation. Included in this total are sums amounting to L1,683,500,000, lent to our Allies and Dominions. For the total casualties of the war, in an earlier chapter I have given the approximate figures so far as they can as yet be ascertained, amounting to at least some *twenty millions*. At such appalling cost then, in death, suffering and that wealth which represents the accumulated labour of men, have the liberties of Europe been rescued from the German attack. We are victors indeed; we have won to the shore; but the wreck of the tempest lies all round us; and what is the future to be?

It is four months now, since, in the splendid rooms of the Villa Murat, I listened to President Wilson describing the sitting of the Conference at which the Resolution was passed constituting the League of Nations—four months big with human fate. The terms of peace are published, and at the present moment no one knows whether Germany will sign them or no. The League of Nations is in existence. It has a home, a Constitution, a Secretariat. But the outlook over Europe is still dark and troubled, and the inner League of Three is still the surest ground in the chaos, the starting-point of the future. The Peace Terms are no final solution—how could they be? On their practical execution, on their adapta-tion year by year to the new world coming into being, all will depend. German militarism has met its doom. The triumph of the Allies is more absolute than any of them could have dreamed four years ago. Nor can the German crime ever be forgotten in this generation, or the German peril ignored. The whole civilised world must be—will be—the shield of France should any fresh outrage threaten her. But after justice comes mercy. Because Germany has shown herself a criminal nation, not all Germans are criminal. That same British Army which as it fought its victorious way through the German defences in the last four months of the war, and, while it fought the enemy, fed and succoured at the same time 800,000 French civilians—men and officers dividing their rations with starving women and children, and in every pause of fighting, spending all their energies in comforting the weak, the hungry, and the sick:— that very Army is sorry now for the German women and children, as it sees them in the German towns. It is our own soldiers who have been demanding food and pity.

The Allies, indeed, have been for some time sending food to their starving enemies. Mr. Hoover—all honour to the great man!—is ceaselessly at work. If only no hitch in the Peace interrupts the food-trains and the incoming ships, so that no more children die!

Some modifications in the Peace Terms would, clearly, be accepted by the public opinion of the Allied countries. No one, I believe, who has seen the Lens district, and the deliberate and cruel destruction of the French industrial north, will feel many qualms about the Saar valley. We may hold a personal opinion that it might have been wiser for France in her own interests to claim the coal only. But it is for France to decide, and it will be for the League of Nations to watch over the solution she has insisted on, in the common interest. But concessions as to Upper Silesia and East Prussia would be received, I have little doubt, with general relief and assent; and the common sense of Europe will certainly see both the wisdom and expediency of setting German industry to work again as speedily as possible, and of so arranging and facilitating the payment of her huge money debt to the Allies that it should not weigh too intolerably on the life of an unborn generation—an innocent generation, who will grow up, as it is, inevitably, under one of the darkest shadows ever cast by history.

Meanwhile now that the just and stern verdict of Europe has been given on the war and its authors, the second and greater half of the Allied task remains. Vast questions are left to the League of Nations, outside the Peace; the re-settlement, politically, of large tracts of Europe; the whole problem of disarmament, involving the future of British and American sea-power; the responsibilities of America in Europe; the economic adjustment of the world. But perhaps the greatest problem of all is the ethical one. How long shall we keep our wrath? Germany has done things in this war which shame civilisation, and seem to make a mockery of all ideas of human progress. But yet!—we must still believe in them; or the sun will go out in heaven. We must still believe that in the long run hatred kills the civilised mind, and to put it at its lowest, is a mortal waste of human energies. Has Christianity, swathed as it is in half-decayed beliefs, any longer power to help us? Yet whatever else in the Christian system is breaking down, the Christian idea of a common fellowship of man holds the field as never before. And both the Christian idea and common sense tell us that till there is again some sort of international life in Europe, Europe will be unsound and her wounds unhealed. We call it impossible. But the good man, the just man, the merciful man is still among us, and—

"What he wills, he does; and does so much That proof is called impossibility."

MARY A. WARD.

ABOUT THE AUTHOR

 **Mary Augusta Ward** (née Arnold; June 11, 1851 – March 26, 1920), was a British novelist who wrote under her married name as Mrs. Humphry Ward.

Mary Augusta Arnold was born in Hobart, Tasmania in 1851. She was the daughter of Tom Arnold, a professor of literature, and Julia Sorrell. Her uncle was the poet Matthew Arnold and her grandfather had been Thomas Arnold, the famous headmaster of Rugby School. Her sister, also called Julia, married Leonard Huxley, the son of Thomas Huxley and their sons were Julian and Aldous Huxley. As a young woman, Mary married Humphry "Thomas" Ward, a writer and editor.

Mary Augusta Ward began her career writing articles for magazines while working on a book for children that was published in 1881 under the title Milly and Olly. Her novels contained strong religious subject matter relevant to Victorian values she herself practised. Her popularity spread beyond Great Britain to the United States. According to the New York Times, her book Lady Rose's Daughter was the bestselling novel in the United States in 1903 as was The Marriage of William Ashe in 1905. Her most popular novel by far was the religious "novel with a purpose" Robert Elsmere, which portrayed the religious crisis of a young pastor and his family.

Choose from Thousands of 1stWorldLibrary Classics By

A. M. Barnard
Ada Leverson
Adolphus William Ward
Aesop
Agatha Christie
Alexander Aaronsohn
Alexander Kielland
Alexandre Dumas
Alfred Gatty
Alfred Ollivant
Alice Duer Miller
Alice Turner Curtis
Alice Dunbar
Allen Chapman
Alleyne Ireland
Ambrose Bierce
Amelia E. Barr
Amory H. Bradford
Andrew Lang
Andrew McFarland Davis
Andy Adams
Angela Brazil
Anna Alice Chapin
Anna Sewell
Annie Besant
Annie Hamilton Donnell
Annie Payson Call
Annie Roe Carr
Annonaymous
Anton Chekhov
Archibald Lee Fletcher
Arnold Bennett
Arthur C. Benson
Arthur Conan Doyle
Arthur M. Winfield
Arthur Ransome
Arthur Schnitzler
Arthur Train
Atticus
B.H. Baden-Powell
B. M. Bower
B. C. Chatterjee
Baroness Emmuska Orczy
Baroness Orczy
Basil King
Bayard Taylor
Ben Macomber
Bertha Muzzy Bower
Bjornstjerne Bjornson

Booth Tarkington
Boyd Cable
Bram Stoker
C. Collodi
C. E. Orr
C. M. Ingleby
Carolyn Wells
Catherine Parr Traill
Charles A. Eastman
Charles Amory Beach
Charles Dickens
Charles Dudley Warner
Charles Farrar Browne
Charles Ives
Charles Kingsley
Charles Klein
Charles Hanson Towne
Charles Lathrop Pack
Charles Romyn Dake
Charles Whibley
Charles Willing Beale
Charlotte M. Braeme
Charlotte M. Yonge
Charlotte Perkins Stetson
Clair W. Hayes
Clarence Day Jr.
Clarence E. Mulford
Clemence Housman
Confucius
Coningsby Dawson
Cornelis DeWitt Wilcox
Cyril Burleigh
D. H. Lawrence
Daniel Defoe
David Garnett
Dinah Craik
Don Carlos Janes
Donald Keyhoe
Dorothy Kilner
Dougan Clark
Douglas Fairbanks
E. Nesbit
E. P. Roe
E. Phillips Oppenheim
E. S. Brooks
Earl Barnes
Edgar Rice Burroughs
Edith Van Dyne
Edith Wharton

Edward Everett Hale
Edward J. O'Biren
Edward S. Ellis
Edwin L. Arnold
Eleanor Atkins
Eleanor Hallowell Abbott
Eliot Gregory
Elizabeth Gaskell
Elizabeth McCracken
Elizabeth Von Arnim
Ellem Key
Emerson Hough
Emilie F. Carlen
Emily Bronte
Emily Dickinson
Enid Bagnold
Enilor Macartney Lane
Erasmus W. Jones
Ernie Howard Pie
Ethel May Dell
Ethel Turner
Ethel Watts Mumford
Eugene Sue
Eugenie Foa
Eugene Wood
Eustace Hale Ball
Evelyn Everett-green
Everard Cotes
F. H. Cheley
F. J. Cross
F. Marion Crawford
Fannie E. Newberry
Federick Austin Ogg
Ferdinand Ossendowski
Fergus Hume
Florence A. Kilpatrick
Fremont B. Deering
Francis Bacon
Francis Darwin
Frances Hodgson Burnett
Frances Parkinson Keyes
Frank Gee Patchin
Frank Harris
Frank Jewett Mather
Frank L. Packard
Frank V. Webster
Frederic Stewart Isham
Frederick Trevor Hill
Frederick Winslow Taylor

Friedrich Kerst
Friedrich Nietzsche
Fyodor Dostoyevsky
G.A. Henty
G.K. Chesterton
Gabrielle E. Jackson
Garrett P. Serviss
Gaston Leroux
George A. Warren
George Ade
Geroge Bernard Shaw
George Cary Eggleston
George Durston
George Ebers
George Eliot
George Gissing
George MacDonald
George Meredith
George Orwell
George Sylvester Viereck
George Tucker
George W. Cable
George Wharton James
Gertrude Atherton
Gordon Casserly
Grace E. King
Grace Gallatin
Grace Greenwood
Grant Allen
Guillermo A. Sherwell
Gulielma Zollinger
Gustav Flaubert
H. A. Cody
H. B. Irving
H.C. Bailey
H. G. Wells
H. H. Munro
H. Irving Hancock
H. R. Naylor
H. Rider Haggard
H. W. C. Davis
Haldeman Julius
Hall Caine
Hamilton Wright Mabie
Hans Christian Andersen
Harold Avery
Harold McGrath
Harriet Beecher Stowe
Harry Castlemon
Harry Coghill
Harry Houidini

Hayden Carruth
Helent Hunt Jackson
Helen Nicolay
Hendrik Conscience
Hendy David Thoreau
Henri Barbusse
Henrik Ibsen
Henry Adams
Henry Ford
Henry Frost
Henry James
Henry Jones Ford
Henry Seton Merriman
Henry W Longfellow
Herbert A. Giles
Herbert Carter
Herbert N. Casson
Herman Hesse
Hildegard G. Frey
Homer
Honore De Balzac
Horace B. Day
Horace Walpole
Horatio Alger Jr.
Howard Pyle
Howard R. Garis
Hugh Lofting
Hugh Walpole
Humphry Ward
Ian Maclaren
Inez Haynes Gillmore
Irving Bacheller
Isabel Cecilia Williams
Isabel Hornibrook
Israel Abrahams
Ivan Turgenev
J.G.Austin
J. Henri Fabre
J. M. Barrie
J. M. Walsh
J. Macdonald Oxley
J. R. Miller
J. S. Fletcher
J. S. Knowles
J. Storer Clouston
J. W. Duffield
Jack London
Jacob Abbott
James Allen
James Andrews
James Baldwin

James Branch Cabell
James DeMille
James Joyce
James Lane Allen
James Lane Allen
James Oliver Curwood
James Oppenheim
James Otis
James R. Driscoll
Jane Abbott
Jane Austen
Jane L. Stewart
Janet Aldridge
Jens Peter Jacobsen
Jerome K. Jerome
Jessie Graham Flower
John Buchan
John Burroughs
John Cournos
John F. Kennedy
John Gay
John Glasworthy
John Habberton
John Joy Bell
John Kendrick Bangs
John Milton
John Philip Sousa
John Taintor Foote
Jonas Lauritz Idemil Lie
Jonathan Swift
Joseph A. Altsheler
Joseph Carey
Joseph Conrad
Joseph E. Badger Jr
Joseph Hergesheimer
Joseph Jacobs
Jules Vernes
Julian Hawthrone
Julie A Lippmann
Justin Huntly McCarthy
Kakuzo Okakura
Karle Wilson Baker
Kate Chopin
Kenneth Grahame
Kenneth McGaffey
Kate Langley Bosher
Kate Langley Bosher
Katherine Cecil Thurston
Katherine Stokes
L. A. Abbot
L. T. Meade

L. Frank Baum
Latta Griswold
Laura Dent Crane
Laura Lee Hope
Laurence Housman
Lawrence Beasley
Leo Tolstoy
Leonid Andreyev
Lewis Carroll
Lewis Sperry Chafer
Lilian Bell
Lloyd Osbourne
Louis Hughes
Louis Joseph Vance
Louis Tracy
Louisa May Alcott
Lucy Fitch Perkins
Lucy Maud Montgomery
Luther Benson
Lydia Miller Middleton
Lyndon Orr
M. Corvus
M. H. Adams
Margaret E. Sangster
Margret Howth
Margaret Vandercook
Margaret W. Hungerford
Margret Penrose
Maria Edgeworth
Maria Thompson Daviess
Mariano Azuela
Marion Polk Angellotti
Mark Overton
Mark Twain
Mary Austin
Mary Catherine Crowley
Mary Cole
Mary Hastings Bradley
Mary Roberts Rinehart
Mary Rowlandson
M. Wollstonecraft Shelley
Maud Lindsay
Max Beerbohm
Myra Kelly
Nathaniel Hawthrone
Nicolo Machiavelli
O. F. Walton
Oscar Wilde

Owen Johnson
P.G. Wodehouse
Paul and Mabel Thorne
Paul G. Tomlinson
Paul Severing
Percy Brebner
Percy Keese Fitzhugh
Peter B. Kyne
Plato
Quincy Allen
R. Derby Holmes
R. L. Stevenson
R. S. Ball
Rabindranath Tagore
Rahul Alvares
Ralph Bonehill
Ralph Henry Barbour
Ralph Victor
Ralph Waldo Emmerson
Rene Descartes
Ray Cummings
Rex Beach
Rex E. Beach
Richard Harding Davis
Richard Jefferies
Richard Le Gallienne
Robert Barr
Robert Frost
Robert Gordon Anderson
Robert L. Drake
Robert Lansing
Robert Lynd
Robert Michael Ballantyne
Robert W. Chambers
Rosa Nouchette Carey
Rudyard Kipling
Saint Augustine
Samuel B. Allison
Samuel Hopkins Adams
Sarah Bernhardt
Sarah C. Hallowell
Selma Lagerlof
Sherwood Anderson
Sigmund Freud
Standish O'Grady
Stanley Weyman
Stella Benson
Stella M. Francis

Stephen Crane
Stewart Edward White
Stijn Streuvels
Swami Abhedananda
Swami Parmananda
T. S. Ackland
T. S. Arthur
The Princess Der Ling
Thomas A. Janvier
Thomas A Kempis
Thomas Anderton
Thomas Bailey Aldrich
Thomas Bulfinch
Thomas De Quincey
Thomas Dixon
Thomas H. Huxley
Thomas Hardy
Thomas More
Thornton W. Burgess
U. S. Grant
Upton Sinclair
Valentine Williams
Various Authors
Vaughan Kester
Victor Appleton
Victor G. Durham
Victoria Cross
Virginia Woolf
Wadsworth Camp
Walter Camp
Walter Scott
Washington Irving
Wilbur Lawton
Wilkie Collins
Willa Cather
Willard F. Baker
William Dean Howells
William le Queux
W. Makepeace Thackeray
William W. Walter
William Shakespeare
Winston Churchill
Yei Theodora Ozaki
Yogi Ramacharaka
Young E. Allison
Zane Grey

www.ingramcontent.com/pod-product-compliance
Lightning Source LLC
Chambersburg PA
CBHW051824170626
46807CB00003B/1023